OUTLAW

By the same author:

The Great Hedge of India
A Brief History of Tea

OUTLAW

India's Bandit Queen and Me

Roy Moxham

RIDER

LONDON   SYDNEY   AUCKLAND   JOHANNESBURG

1 3 5 7 9 10 8 6 4 2

First published in 2010 by Rider, an imprint of Ebury Publishing

Ebury Publishing is a Random House Group company

The Random House Group Limited Reg. No. 954009

Addresses for companies within the Random House Group can be found at
www.rbooks.co.uk

A CIP catalogue record for this book is available from the British Library

The Random House Group Limited supports The Forest Stewardship
Council (FSC), the leading international forest certification organisation.
All our titles that are printed on Greenpeace approved FSC certified paper
carry the FSC logo. Our paper procurement policy can be found at
www.rbooks.co.uk/environment

Mixed Sources
Product group from well-managed
forests and other controlled sources
www.fsc.org Cert no. TT-COC-2139
© 1996 Forest Stewardship Council

FSC

Printed and bound in Great Britain by Clays Ltd, St Ives plc

ISBN 9781846041822

Copies are available at special rates for bulk orders. Contact the sales
development team on 020 7840 8487 for more information.

To buy books by your favourite authors and register for offers, visit
www.rbooks.co.uk

Contents

List of Illustrations

Charts and maps

Black and white plates

With the exception of images 1, 15 and 16, all photographs are copyright of Roy Moxham.

1. Phoolan Devi formally surrenders at Bhind, 12 February 1983 (© *Sondeep Shankar/AP/Press Association Images*).

2. The author in front of Phoolan Devi's family home. Ghura ka Purva, 1996.

3. Ramkali, Phoolan's younger sister, milking the water-buffalo. Ghura ka Purva, 1996.

4. Phoolan Devi's first letter to the author, dated 29 June 1992.

5. Photograph of Phoolan copied on to her letter to the author from Gwalior Jail, dated 16 October 1992. Her signature is underneath.

6. Phoolan Devi with the author, covered in pigment, at Holi. Delhi, 1994.

7. Shiv Narayan, Phoolan Devi's brother, with his wife, Shoba. Gwalior, 1993.

8. Munni, Phoolan's youngest sister, at the family shrine. Gulmohar Park, Delhi, 1995.

PHOOLAN DEVI'S FAMILY TREE

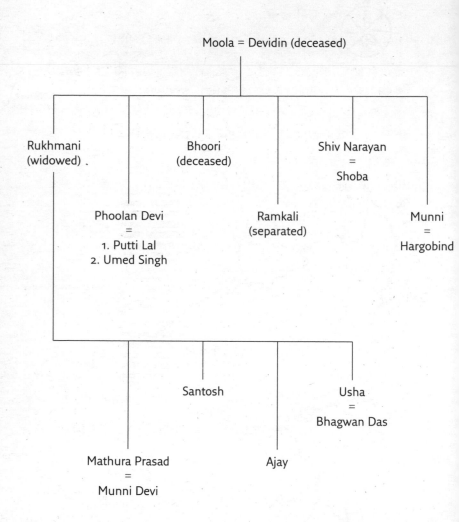

Moola = Devidin (deceased)

Rukhmani (widowed)

Bhoori (deceased)

Shiv Narayan = Shoba

Phoolan Devi
=
1. Putti Lal
2. Umed Singh

Ramkali (separated)

Munni
=
Hargobind

Santosh

Usha
=
Bhagwan Das

Mathura Prasad
=
Munni Devi

Ajay

THE STATE OF UTTAR PRADESH

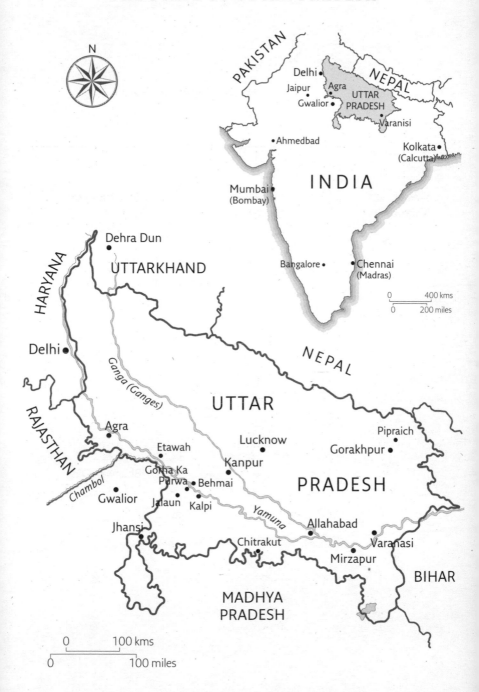

A Letter from India

1
A Letter from India

'If I am released alive, then I will surely meet you …
If I die, then in my next birth.'

IN JUNE 1992 I did a very strange thing. I wrote to a bandit in an Indian jail. In the *Independent* the previous day there had been an article about Phoolan Devi, the 'Bandit Queen'. It was prompted by her standing as a candidate in a by-election to the Indian parliament. She wanted to draw attention to her own plight and also to give the Indian poor, the lower castes and 'Untouchables', a voice, particularly women. Apparently, she had surrendered to the authorities after being accused of killing twenty-two upper-caste landowners who had raped her, but though it was agreed that she would be released after no more than eight years in jail, this had not happened. She was still in prison. I had never heard of her before but was immediately struck by the harshness of her life, much of it spent in wild ravines, and by her determination to do something about it – both for herself and for others.

This impulsive gesture was so unlike me. Why did I do it? I suppose that my first visit to India in February had been such a shock. Hiring an auto-rickshaw from Mumbai (Bombay) airport to the city centre, I had been taken on a 'short cut' through India's biggest slum. A population of a million or more in pathetic makeshift huts had no proper water supply or sewage system. Children in rags and pigs playing in open cesspits. There was an overpowering smell of filth.

The hostel I stayed in was not far from the luxurious Taj Mahal Hotel. This was surrounded by fabulously expensive jewellers and boutiques, which for the most part catered not to tourists, but to Indians. Rich Indians were driven there in expensive imported cars. The contrast between the lives of the rich and the poor was the same in many other cities. In the villages, the poor were even poorer. It became obvious to me that India had no shortage of money; it needed no overseas aid. The problem was in how its wealth was distributed.

Since that first visit, I had been looking for something that I could do to make an impact. I gave a little money to charities but really I knew that political power for the poor, the majority of Indians, was what was needed. So, with that in mind, and perhaps for other reasons that I was never fully able to explain, I sent Phoolan Devi a letter of support. I offered some help with her legal fees if needed. I also enclosed a postcard of the Houses of Parliament with 'good luck' written on the back. Having no proper address, I sent it by recorded delivery, with an international reply coupon, to:

Phoolan Devi
c/o The Governor
Gwalior Jail
Madhya Pradesh
India

I wondered, would she get it? Would she reply?

A few days later the newspapers reported that Phoolan Devi had lost the by-election in Delhi, and her deposit of 500 rupees (£11). The other two candidates were film stars. A political party that represented those at the very bottom of Indian society had backed Phoolan's campaign. I was glad that I had sent my letter since it must have been a bad setback for her.

That weekend I was browsing in Hatchard's Bookshop when I came across *India's Bandit Queen – the True Story of Phoolan Devi* by Mala Sen. I stayed up reading it until 2 a.m., completely gripped. What a story. There were good photographs of Phoolan Devi, her family and of various bandits.

*

It seemed that Phoolan Devi had been born into a very poor low-caste family in a village in the north-central Indian state of Uttar Pradesh. Unable to raise an attractive dowry, her parents married her off when only eleven to Putti Lal, a man in a distant village. He was twenty years older than her. He continually beat her, and sexually molested her even though she had not reached puberty. After three years of this, she became ill and he returned her 'in disgrace' to her family. Social stigma forced her family to return her to the husband. He, meanwhile, had acquired another woman. The two of them treated her as a slave – beating and starving her for several years – before returning her once again to her village. This time she was allowed to stay.

In the village, Phoolan became embroiled in a conflict with some richer relatives over family land. They arranged for bandits to kidnap her. Despite asking for police protection she was abducted. The gang was led by one Babu Singh, who made it clear that he wanted Phoolan as his mistress. One of the gang, Vikram Singh Mallah, who came from the same low caste as Phoolan, then killed the high-caste Babu Singh and Phoolan became his mistress.

The gang – now all low-caste – carried out many raids. They were based in the wild ravines of the Chambal river valley. Dressed as police, they ventured out to stop trucks and rob landowners. They took money from the rich and bought support from the poor. Eventually, knowing that now she could never return to her village, Phoolan joined in.

Vikram's gang joined up with an upper-caste gang. They seemed friendly but it was a ruse. Vikram and many of his men were shot. Phoolan was captured, confined in a village called Behmai, and constantly raped. Eventually, a sympathetic priest smuggled a shotgun into her and she escaped.

Phoolan Devi then met with the gang of one of Vikram's friends. They united together with a bandit called Man Singh, and formed a new gang that Phoolan would command. After some time, Man Singh and Phoolan became lovers. This gang carried out many raids in both Uttar Pradesh and the adjacent state of Madhya Pradesh. In one notorious incident they captured a town, looted the bazaar and distributed the goods to the poor. Phoolan became a folk hero. The government offered a reward for her, dead or alive.

In 1981 the gang attacked Behmai, where Phoolan had been imprisoned and raped. Twenty-two upper-caste villagers were rounded up and shot. Although Phoolan denied being directly involved in the massacre, she became the most wanted suspect. The government mobilised thousands of police to catch her. They tortured, raped and killed many innocent people. Phoolan, with the aid of the lower castes that she had always taken pains to help, evaded capture. In the wake of this and other reverses, the Chief Minister of Uttar Pradesh (politically the most important state in India, with the huge population of 140 million) was forced to resign.

The Prime Minister of India, Mrs Indira Gandhi, then authorised the Madhya Pradesh police to negotiate a surrender deal. Eventually an agreement was concluded whereby none of the gang would be kept in jail for longer than eight years. In February 1983, Phoolan and her men ceremonially surrendered to the Chief Minister of Madhya Pradesh. Without ever appearing in front of a court, they were taken to Gwalior Jail.

(According to Mala Sen's book, Phoolan was twenty-six when she was jailed, which would make her about thirty-five in

1992. The *Independent* article had put her age at thirty-two. Later in her life, most reports dated her birth as 10 August 1963. This would have made her only nineteen at her surrender and imprisonment, and still in her twenties when I first wrote to her in 1992. Earlier reports put the year of her birth as 1957. Exactly when she was born is unclear.)

I had some vague knowledge of the Hindu caste system but, as it appeared to figure prominently in Phoolan's story, I read more about it. There were four main caste divisions. At the top were the Brahmins, traditionally the priestly caste. Below them were the Kshatriyas, originally the rulers and warriors, now the main landowners. In some parts of India they were called Rajputs; in Uttar Pradesh they were known as Thakurs. Below them were the Vaishyas, the merchants and farmers. At the bottom were the Sudras, to which Phoolan belonged, the labourers. Each of these main castes had a multitude of sub-castes, often confusingly themselves described as castes. Phoolan, for example, was from the Mallah, the sub-caste originally composed of boatmen and their families. Even lower than the Sudras were the Dalits or Untouchables, who were assigned to 'unclean' work. In the cities the caste system was beginning to break down, but in the countryside it remained largely intact. To a large extent the upper castes were the wealthy and the lower castes the poor. In theory it was possible to escape the caste system by converting to another religion, but even then the stigma of a low-caste origin tended to linger.

*

On 30 June I received a postcard from India, an 'Advice of Delivery'. It had a Gwalior postal stamp. There was a signature on it that looked like it might be in Hindi script. Of course, I could not read it, so I did not know whether it was Phoolan Devi's.

A fortnight later a letter from India arrived, written in what I
assumed was Hindi. The signature was in a different hand, the
same as on the earlier postcard. I needed someone to do a
translation. This posed a problem, since it seems that Phoolan
Devi was so hated by many Indians that I could get myself into
serious trouble – perhaps even be attacked. Although seen as a
Robin Hood figure by the poor, who idolised her, the wealthy
upper castes saw her as a criminal and a dangerous threat to
their traditional power. By chance, my friends Nick and Helen
came round to my flat in the evening. Helen, who was teaching
in London, said that one of the teachers she worked with knew
Hindi. We photocopied the letter and Helen said she would ask
her colleague if she would translate it.

At that time, I was working as a book and paper conservator
for the Passmore Edwards Museum in East London. There had
been a fire in West Ham Town Hall. This, and the water used
to extinguish it, had severely damaged the archives of the old
borough. Parish registers, including those recording the deaths
in the plague of 1665, had been particularly affected. I had been
engaged on a five-year contract to save the most important
items. One evening, later in that week when I received
Phoolan's letter, a group of us from the museum went for a
colleague's leaving-party meal in Brick Lane. We met up in
a pub. Before we went on to the Clifton restaurant, I nipped
across the road to a cafe full of Asians. I asked if anyone knew
Hindi and managed to find a man to look through the copied
letter. He told me that it was from Phoolan herself. She wrote
that she was grateful for my message, as she was very
depressed. The letter then went on about how badly women
were treated in India. The translator, and the men gathered
around him, began to look angry. I made my excuses and
rushed off. I needed a proper translation quickly. Unfortunately
Helen's colleague was away, so I would need to wait for
anything from her. At supper, one of my museum colleagues,

Nerina, told me that her aunt had a friend who might help. I gave her the copied letter to see what she could do.

Next week Nerina came to see me.

'I gave the letter to my aunt,' she told me. 'She was with a friend from India, who has fluent Hindi. When this friend started to translate, she came to a sentence – "I curse God that I was born in India!" My aunt then leapt out of her chair, grabbed the letter, and shredded it!'

That same day, I received a phone call from the archivist at Canterbury Cathedral offering me the conservator's post that I had recently been interviewed for. I was delighted, since it was such an amazing archive and it would be wonderful to be working on such important medieval documents. They seemed to be keen to have me too, and wanted me to begin earlier than we had discussed. I agreed to start mid-September. I also managed to get the archivist to honour my 'holiday arrangements' so that I could go to India over Christmas. Perhaps, I thought, I could meet Phoolan. That would be really something.

The translation of Phoolan Devi's letter by Helen's colleague was further delayed by the onset of the school holidays. This was very frustrating. Throwing caution to the winds, I decided to try the Indian restaurant at the end of my road, where they seemed friendly. I photocopied the letter but, to keep it anonymous, without the signature. A young waiter there, Ajit, who seemed very well educated, offered to translate it for me. He immediately exclaimed, 'This is from Phoolan Devi!' Apparently it started off 'to Mr Roy from Phoolan.' So much for my attempt at concealment. Actually, both he and the other staff turned out to be very sympathetic to her and very supportive of my efforts. I thought that this was probably because they were Sikhs. Following the assassination of the Indian Prime Minister, Indira Gandhi, in 1984 by her Sikh bodyguards, the Sikhs had been treated badly by Indian governments. They tended to be sympathetic to others who had been discriminated against. I discovered later that the restaurant owner was active in Amnesty International. Whatever the reason, they insisted on giving me free beer.

The letter was from Gwalior Jail, dated 29 June 1992:

Hail God

To Mr Roy from Phoolan – a lot of thanks.

Received your letter – I felt so happy I cannot express it in words. It is very good of you to have given respect to a woman like me. I am myself helpless and destitute – whatever I had was spent in the election. I don't have a rupee for court fees. In India lawyers are very costly. Also in India no one listens to women. Nobody cares to give them justice. Sometimes, I curse God that I was born in a place like India. When I die, I shall be reborn in London, or some other such place, where women are given equality. Due to being a woman I am not able to get justice. I don't think I shall ever receive justice.

I request that you help me as much as possible. I should be grateful if you could print an appeal in the press there – that all brothers and sisters donate 'just one day's cigarette money' to help a desolate woman like me. It would be very kind and helpful. I can then fight against the injustice being done to me – to any woman.

I know you will definitely help me. I received your letter at a time when I had lost all hope in life. At such a time, reading your letter gave me the will to live. That is all. My heartfelt good wishes to you and your friends. Whoever wants to send something should send it to the address below:

My address: Phoolan Devi Nishad
               Self Surrendered Dacoit
               Central Jail
               Gwalior
               M. P.

Please reply at the earliest. Anybody sending anything should write to the jail address by registered post – otherwise the jail officials play their tricks.

Phoolan Devi

The Indian Government has done great injustice to me.

The signature was in a different hand, which I assumed was hers. I imagined, therefore, that she had to get someone to write the letter on her behalf because she was illiterate. I was elated to have received such a reply, especially such a forceful one. I resolved to do my best to help her and to try and find some money for a lawyer. I would also make sure that I wrote to her regularly so that she felt she had some support.

I wondered again why I had written to a woman in an Indian jail. There were vaguely political reasons, but maybe others too. I had sometimes thought that my life, compared with that of others I had met, had been rather mundane. When I voiced this to friends, most looked astounded. I had begun to realise that, viewed dispassionately, my life had been far from ordinary. I had also begun to realise that I had a strong streak of romanticism.

I remembered that in 1960, when I was only twenty, I had put an advertisement in *The Times* seeking a post on a tea or tobacco estate. Given that I had no connections with that world, and indeed had never met anyone with knowledge of it, it was a quixotic act. Nevertheless, things worked out well for me. I received only one response and became a tea planter in Malawi (then Nyasaland). After a few very enjoyable years, I joined a company marketing agricultural machinery. With them, I subsequently moved to Kenya and Tanzania. I travelled all over those beautiful countries, living in romantic locations such as Dar es Salaam and Kilimanjaro. I liked to boast that I had driven along every road in those countries. I was in eastern Africa for thirteen happy years.

Similarly, in the 1970s, I had established a shop in London to sell African art. True, I was interested in art, but actually, I now realised, it had been largely to provide a vehicle for me to travel that continent more widely. It was the love of travelling not the love of art that drove me. I visited most countries in Africa, often buying a one-way ticket to somewhere in west or east Africa and then travelling back overland.

Foreign places, especially those in the tropics, held a strong fascination for me. Why I should have felt this pull – alone in my family and among my school-friends – was a mystery. For someone brought up in a quiet town in Worcestershire, by a widowed mother who had run a shop selling knitting paraphernalia, it was a strange obsession.

Financial pressures forced me into a settled life in London. I went to college for the first time in the late 1970s. Close to my fortieth birthday, I graduated as a book and paper conservator. (Even choosing that offbeat occupation had an element of romanticism. I had found a pile of dilapidated old books in a skip on Southampton Row, purchased them from the men clearing the building for £5, and sold most of them for quite a lot of money. I then enrolled in an evening class in book restoration in order to repair the remainder as a keepsake. I enjoyed the novelty of working with my hands and decided to pursue conservation as a career.) Throughout the 1980s I hardly travelled. At the beginning of that decade, busy with my new career, I was happy to be in London, with the occasional visit to friends in Spain. By the end of the decade, however, I was more restless. I longed to revisit the tropics. My trip to India in early 1992 had resuscitated my love affair and I was keen to engage again with the exotic.

*

I sent out a résumé of Phoolan's life, together with an appeal for support, to a few close friends. I wanted to be able to tell Phoolan that others here besides me were concerned for her welfare. However, not everyone, I supposed, would be as enthusiastic as I was to give help to a jailed bandit. It would be interesting to see who responded.

Helen's colleague finally sent her translation. This was much the same as Ajit's. Various friends promised small donations, which pleased me. Some friends seemed to find it hard to relate to Phoolan's story. It was so far from their own experience that it was as though they saw it as fiction. Or perhaps not even so realistic as that. One friend in particular switched our conversation about Phoolan to the latest episode of *The Archers*. He became so emotionally involved in what had happened in that radio serial that it was obvious to me, surprising though that was, that he found it more realistic than a real event.

One friend made a half-joking remark about my writing to a young Indian woman. I angrily rebutted the insinuation. When I first wrote to Phoolan Devi it had not struck me that my motives might be misconstrued. I regarded older men who went to south-east Asia for sex with young women as repulsive. It had not crossed my mind that I might be seen in the same category, even though I was at least twenty years older than her. Perhaps this was partly because I knew from pictures I had seen that Phoolan was not particularly good-looking. In Mala Sen's book the photographs of her showed a woman with rather coarse features. I had come across another book about Phoolan – *Devi: The Bandit Queen* by Richard Shears and Isobelle Gidley, published in 1984. It contained some particularly unflattering photographs of Phoolan. Moreover, it contained a reproduction of an artist's impression that the police had used when they were trying to capture her. This photograph was of a much more attractive woman. Apparently it was based on the features of Phoolan's sister Ramkali, the family beauty. This error had enabled Phoolan to pass close to police officers and remain unnoticed. Certainly, at her surrender, Phoolan's plain features had been a disappointment to many. Of course, when I wrote that first letter to her I had no idea what she looked like. Later, had she been more beautiful, I might perhaps have had second thoughts about our future relationship. As it was, I thought of her as if I were some kind of relative, unlikely as that was. This was made easier, although it was common usage in India, by her signing herself as my sister.

*

I sent off a registered letter to Phoolan with postal orders for £100. Goodness only knows how she would manage to cash postal orders from jail. I also enclosed a postcard of Canterbury Cathedral, telling her that I would start my new job as archive conservator there next month. I imagined that to her it would seem a very strange occupation.

In September, I received a letter in poor English from a Dr Abdul Majid.

Aerogramme from Delhi, dated 1 September 1992:

With the name of God merciful & beneficent.

Dear Brother,

Adab (I respect you)

I am well here and hope you are also quite well. You do not know me and I am writing you letter so I define myself. I am Dr Abdul Majid and Phoolan Devi's brother. Phoolan do not know English and you are Englandian, so I am replying.

First of all we are grateful and thanking you have sympathy for Phoolan in favour of humanity. We are also grateful and thanking to every gentleman and lady of London who have given place in their hearts and respect to Phoolan as brave woman, not remember as a robber. This sentence gave great satisfaction after reading your letter. Unfortunately Phoolan

Devi's enemies and their relatives are more in number in cabinet of ruling team in India.

In this condition we feel very unsafety for Phoolan out of jail. Though she is in jail in present but I think day and night how I can safe her if she will be relieved from jail in future. We have not any overseas journey in our life, so we demand your mercy more and more.

I do not know so good English, so neglect my writing errors. I will send Phoolan's photograph in next letter because envelope for overseas mail is not available this time in my city. Please write about your profession also. I am addressless nowadays. I am also fighting against criminals and social exploiters.

Yours,

Dr Abdul Majid

He asked for a reply to be sent both to Phoolan in Gwalior and to himself care of a schoolteacher in Uttar Pradesh.

I was shocked, as it had not occurred to me that Phoolan's life would be in danger if she was set free. There was, of course, little likelihood of her being allowed to enter Britain. There would not be much point in my aiding her release if she was then to be killed. Nevertheless, in her own letter she had seemed very keen to get out of prison. She must have considered the consequences, I reasoned, so I decided to go along with that.

I sent off a reply to Dr Majid. I told him that the British government was unlikely to let Phoolan stay here as a refugee. I suggested that a lawyer might be able to obtain an undertaking from the Indian government to give her protection when she was released. I asked if he knew whether Phoolan had received the postal orders. I also asked if he knew whether she had engaged a lawyer and that if she had, to send me the name and address.

In October, nearly two months after sending off the postal orders, I wrote to Phoolan, to say that I'd had no response and that I was wondering whether she had received the money. I asked her for the name and address of her lawyer. I told her about the letter from Abdul Majid and enclosed a copy of my reply. I reiterated that she was unlikely to get permission to come to Britain as a refugee.

I booked a flight to Delhi. A number of years of self-employment had left my finances in a precarious position. Since starting at the museum and then moving to Canterbury, my situation had improved, but I still had to be careful with money. Fortunately, once in India, it was possible to live very cheaply. Nevertheless, I needed to select an inexpensive flight, so I took the lowest priced that I could find, which was by Aeroflot. This involved flying via Moscow. I was to leave in mid-December for five weeks.

Early in November, I returned from Canterbury to my flat in London, where I lived at weekends, to find a letter from Phoolan. The notepaper had a black-and-white picture of her photocopied into the corner. She seemed to be amazingly resourceful for someone in jail. I was pleased to see that the photograph showed a cheerful-looking woman with a round face and a broad smile. It seemed that the scowling young woman in many of the photographs taken at her surrender had been transformed. Her appearance was almost homely. In the midst of the Hindi writing there was an advocate's address written in English. I took the letter to Ajit at the Indian restaurant and he dropped by later with a translation.

The letter was from Gwalior Jail and dated 16 October 1992:

Victory to Goddess Durga

Mr Roy,

Greetings to Mr Moxham Roy. I am well here and pray to God that you are too. I am sorry for the delay in writing. The letter and the money you sent me have got into the jail officials' hands. I signed for the registered letter but they would not hand it over to me. They say they have to make enquiries before giving it to me. But do not worry, I will get the money from them.

I have engaged a lawyer. There are some other great men like you who are helping me. You are really wonderful – I respect you, and consider you as an elder brother. If everyone here were as good as you there would be no atrocities against poor women. However, India is a male-dominated country. Here the men can commit any tyranny and yet be pardoned. But a woman is punished severely even for a small mistake and people regard her with contempt. Men then do what they want with them and afterwards accuse them of being bad.

In a country like India, where men rule, women are not respected and are second-class citizens.

I am thinking of changing my religion. What religion do you think I should embrace so that I can attain salvation?

You ask me who is Dr Majid. Well, he is just like an elder brother to me. You may also receive another letter, from my elder sister Mala Sen – I regard her as my sister – who has written my life-story.

I am really grateful to you, and pin a lot of hope on you. Give my greetings to your wife, parents and friends. I am sending this photograph to you – please send me yours.

Here is my lawyer's address. Please write to her saying 'Get justice for Phoolan Devi.'

Ms Kamini Jaiswal, Supreme Court Advocate
[An address in New Delhi with telephone numbers was inserted in English.]

Please forgive any mistakes in this letter.

In this place the officials are not straight. They can do anything behind your back. But, if they do not give me the money, I'll

file a petition in the High Court. I have learnt that the total was
Rs 5,300. I pray to God that you come into lots of money and
will be able to help a poor woman like me.

Please reply soon, your sister,

Phoolan Devi

It was such an emotive letter that I immediately decided to
try to visit Phoolan in Gwalior Jail. I had already planned an
itinerary for my India visit, but that could be altered. I desperately wanted to see what she was really like. Would she be as
plain-speaking and as lacking in artifice as her letters suggested?
I had the impression that, although illiterate, she was highly
intelligent. Nevertheless, she seemed to welcome advice.

I wrote to Phoolan's lawyer, Kamini Jaiswal, enclosing a copy
of Phoolan's letter so that she knew the background. I asked her
if we could meet in Delhi the following month and whether she
could arrange for me to visit Phoolan in jail. I also wrote back to
Phoolan. I told her that I had written to her lawyer, but did not
mention that I was coming to India. I did not want to disappoint
her if I could not obtain permission for a visit.

I thanked her for her photograph and enclosed one of myself
– repairing a medieval manuscript. I also told her that I could
not advise her about religion since, although I was working
at Canterbury Cathedral, I was not particularly religious. No
doubt she would think that very peculiar.

I had not been impressed with the Christianity of many at
Canterbury Cathedral. When I first reported for duty a colleague
had come to take me through the impressive medieval entrance
into the precincts. 'You are now passing through Christ Church
Gate,' he said, 'you are now leaving Christianity behind to
discover Religion.'

And so it proved. I was not a practising Christian. (I had been
brought up as a Catholic, but long ago ceased to attend that
Church, and had moved towards pantheism – which had made
me sympathetic to some aspects of Hinduism.) Nevertheless, I

had developed a respect for the impecunious clergy I had encountered in London. They did much for the unfortunate. Canterbury was another world, where the clergy mostly lived in a grand style. I shared a house with virgers and organ scholars, who gave me all the gossip. They doubted whether some of clergy even believed in God. There were many tales of arrogant and unchristian behaviour. A clergyman who was referred to with affection was the long-dead Hewlett Johnson, the bane of the establishment, the 'Red Dean'. He had shown local people many kindnesses. A Christian communist, it was he who had invited Gandhi to Canterbury Cathedral. Gandhi had gone to evening service, only for the ceremony to be boycotted by the other clergy.

*

A week before I was due to leave for India, there was bad news. A Hindu mob had destroyed a sixteenth-century mosque at Ayodhya in Uttar Pradesh state. They had claimed that it was built on the site of a demolished Hindu temple that marked the birthplace of the Hindu god-king, Lord Ram. They wanted to rebuild that temple. It had been a *cause célèbre* of the Hindu nationalist party, the upper-caste-dominated BJP, for many years. Muslims were incensed. Riots had broken out across India. Central government had taken control of Uttar Pradesh and curfews were in force in many states. I wondered if I should cancel my flight. I was very reluctant to do that, since I would not get a refund and could not afford to re-book, and I was very keen to meet Phoolan, to find out what she was really like. I decided to leave it for a couple of days to see if things might calm down. Three days later the Indian government seemed to have the situation under reasonable control, although there were still curfews. These would make travelling difficult, but I decided to go ahead anyway. I flew out of London on 13 December.

2
Jail

'Get me released as soon as possible –
otherwise I may die here.'

MY JOURNEY to India did not go smoothly. The propeller plane left late and was then diverted because of bad weather. When we finally arrived at Moscow we had missed our connecting flight, and we were rescheduled for the following day. The airport was a dingy shambles. We tried to sleep in the departure lounge but were chased out by soldiers who bedded down there themselves. Fortunately an Indian musician who had been playing in Paris took out his sarangi, which looked like a small cello, and treated us to a wonderful recital. The plaintive music, uncannily like a human voice, was very appropriate. I shared with him some whisky that I was carrying and he urged me to visit him in Jaipur. We finally reached Delhi at midnight – not a good time, as I had no hotel reservation. I took a bus into town.

New Delhi, the Imperial capital built by the British earlier in the century, was seven miles to the north-east of the airport. For the first few miles the narrow road wove through a hotch-potch of unpretentious shops and hotels, their potholed fore-courts deep in litter. Then we sped up deserted grand avenues, lined with magnificent trees. Peeping from behind them were huge colonial bungalows set in vast gardens. Occasionally I spotted the silhouette of a crumbling fort or tomb from an earlier empire. Further on, I was dropped off near the circular main shopping complex of Connaught Place. There was no sign of a curfew. It was my first visit to Delhi and I was surprised by the cold. Unlike balmy Mumbai, Delhi was, as I then remembered, well north of the tropics. There were clusters of people sleeping on the pavements and many had lit bonfires to keep warm. The air was full of smoke. With some effort, I found a small hotel above some shops with a not too expensive room.

*

I slept in until 9 a.m. and then rang Kamini Jaiswal. She said that she had received my letter and would see me at 6 p.m. It was now quite warm under a cloudless, but hazy with pollution, blue sky. I moved into a cheaper hotel in the Paharganj area, just north of Connaught Place. Although the two locations were within walking distance, they were completely different. Paharganj was extraordinarily crowded. Cycle-rickshaws, cars and lorries eased their way through the crush of bodies. The narrow streets of shops were lined with market stalls selling fruit and vegetables, snacks and drinks. Cows wandered between the stalls as they searched for fodder. The air smelt of spices and urine.

I tried to visit the nearby Red Fort but the road was closed by a curfew. It was difficult to find out exactly what travel restrictions were in force. I checked the newspapers and asked various travel agents and travellers. The situation did appear to be improving. I gathered, however, that quite a few towns were still under a twenty-four-hour curfew. One of them was Varanasi, so it looked like I would have to postpone that visit.

Kamini Jaiswal's office was in south Delhi, in a clean and sedate residential area, on the top floor of a smart modern house. She was in conservative Indian dress and perhaps in her late thirties. Seated behind her desk in a room lined with leather-backed legal books, she looked quite severe. At first she was rather hostile, querulously asking why there was so much foreign interest in Phoolan Devi. A German TV station wanted to do a series of interviews with Phoolan. Soon, however, she mellowed and ordered tea. She told me that it was Mala Sen who had asked her to help Phoolan. She was not taking a fee. Phoolan, I gathered, was not an easy client to represent. She was suspicious of everyone, even Kamini. Some dubious local lawyers were trying to take over the case for their own ends. It was not that unusual, she told me, for people to be in jail without ever having gone through the courts. There might be ten thousand such persons in Indian jails, and she had represented a number.

The main obstacles stopping Phoolan's release, Kamini told me, were the charges against her in Uttar Pradesh. Phoolan had surrendered in Madhya Pradesh because she had felt that the police there could be trusted. The Uttar Pradesh police had a reputation for extra-judicial executions. However, the Madhya Pradesh amnesty did not apply in Uttar Pradesh. In that state, which borders on Madhya Pradesh, Phoolan faced seventy outstanding counts of murder and banditry. Most of these carried the death penalty. Kamini was trying to have them quashed because of the long delay in bringing the cases to court.

Kamini suggested that I postpone any attempt to visit the jail, as just then the authorities were preoccupied with the general security situation. She proposed that I contact her again when I returned to Delhi in early January. I agreed with her that this might be best. It was something of a disappointment but, with any luck, things would soon calm down.

I left Delhi on 17 December and travelled to Udaipur, Pushkar and Jaipur (where I looked up the sarangi player who was at Moscow airport: despite being poor, he and his family were delighted to see me and most hospitable), Agra, Allahabad and Mirzapur.

Mirzapur was a scruffy little town in Uttar Pradesh, on the banks of the River Ganges. In the early nineteenth century it had been the last port on the river that was deep enough to take steamships. This had made the town an important trading centre. The coming of the railways later in the century brought this prosperity to an end. The town's prestigious buildings fell into disuse. Its fine houses became neglected.

Mirzapur was, however, still famous for its temple. This, a few miles outside the town, was dedicated to an aspect of the goddess Durga, Vindhyavasini Devi. It had long been a popular destination for pilgrims, especially outlaws. I climbed up the hill to the temple through a crowed alley full of stalls selling religious paraphernalia – marigold and hibiscus flowers, coconuts, tasselled cloths stencilled with the name of the goddess and pictures of the goddess herself. The temple was a modern concrete structure, resembling a bus shelter. I offered up my coconut to the priest, who smashed it open at the base of the ancient statue. The goddess was decorated with multiple strings of flowers, so that only her frightening black face with its huge white eyes was visible. The throng behind me soon pushed me on. As I went back down the hill to my auto-rickshaw I bought a picture of the goddess to take to Phoolan. Her letters had been headed with an invocation to Durga. It seemed appropriate that Phoolan should have a special attachment to the goddess who was usually depicted as riding a tiger, with weapons to fight evil in each hand. I was told that the temple was used by dacoits (from *dakait*, Hindi for bandit), so I assumed that she knew of it, or may even have visited it before she was jailed.

So far on my travels I had encountered no curfews. I then went on to Varanasi, where a bomb at New Year had injured many. A curfew from 9 p.m. until dawn was in force. The overwhelming religious atmosphere affected me and I found myself floating a posy of marigolds and roses down the River Ganges for Phoolan's release.

At the beginning of January I telephoned Kamini Jaiswal to tell her that I would return from Varanasi to Delhi on the 8th. She was very friendly. She suggested that I visit her on that evening so that she could give me directions as to how to find Phoolan's relatives in Gwalior.

The journey back to Delhi was difficult as I had to wait eight hours for my train and then it was cancelled. I had to bribe a conductor to get me on to the following train. I reached Delhi mid-afternoon, checked into a Paharganj hotel, cleaned up after the long journey and rushed off to see Kamini Jaiswal. She had just returned from Gwalior.

Kamini had discovered that although all the charges against Phoolan in Madhya Pradesh had been dropped, she had not been freed because of instructions from Central Government. This had enabled an action for her release to be mounted in the Indian Supreme Court in Delhi. Kamini Jaiswal thought this was a welcome development.

Kamini gave me detailed instructions on how to find the house of Phoolan's brother in Gwalior. She told me that she was hoping to come to Britain in the summer and I invited her to visit me at Canterbury Cathedral.

*

Two days after my meeting with Kamini Jaiswal, I took the morning train to Gwalior. It was a five-hour journey, but in a comfortable air-conditioned carriage. The padded armchairs reminded me of those on British Airways planes in their luxurious heyday. One of the disadvantages in travelling in air-conditioned class, however, was that the windows tended to be dirty. It felt as though you were observing India on an antique TV screen. Nevertheless, as we travelled between Agra and Gwalior and crossed the Chambal River, I could make out the ravines where Phoolan and her gang had hidden. It was a landscape of crumbling rock and sand with a few scrub trees. The ravines were shallower than I had imagined – maybe two hundred feet deep – but there were row upon row of them, interlinked and stretching to the horizon. This went on for mile after mile. I could see how easy it would be to hide in them and escape capture. Nevertheless, it was a tribute to Phoolan's extraordinary skill in this terrain that in the aftermath of the Behmai massacre she had managed to evade the thousands of police combing the ravines for her. There was an army officer in the carriage. He pointed out of the window and said, 'This is dacoit country – keep an eye on your luggage!'

At Gwalior, I checked into a hotel and immediately set off to find Phoolan's brother's house while it was still light. The town was dominated by a massive hill-fort, which must have been two miles long. The taxi wended along the narrow streets beneath it until we were on the edge of the town. I saw a sign to the Central Prison. We passed an avenue leading to it, but I could not see much of the building. Further on, we left the road to go down deeply rutted tracks to a cluster of police flats and houses. We were guided to a small ground-floor flat. Phoolan's brother was not living there but a woman, who I thought might be Phoolan's sister, directed my driver to his flat. This was a couple of miles away.

We found the police tenement block and the flat easily enough. A rather glamorous woman who was the brother's wife, Shoba, opened the door. She told us that Shiv Narayan was on duty. (The surrender agreement stipulated that Phoolan's young and only brother should receive free education and then a government job. He was now a police constable.) Shoba spoke some English and invited me in. I was introduced to Phoolan's mother, Moola. She was a tiny woman with a serene smile, who showed little sign of her tumultuous life. I arranged to return at eleven the following morning, when Shiv Narayan would be off duty.

*

Next morning I arrived on schedule at Shiv Narayan's. He was in his twenties, slim and good-looking, with a small moustache. He had very little English and had no idea what I could be doing there until I showed him Phoolan's letter. He became friendlier when he realised that I was not a journalist. Unfortunately, he was due back on duty at midday, so we arranged to meet in the evening at my hotel. He said he would try to bring someone to translate. There was only one room in the police flat, but it was well furnished and relatively prosperous-looking, with both TV and air-conditioner. I took a photo of the couple (the mother had gone) looking very smart. Shiv Narayan was in a neatly pressed police uniform, khaki trousers and olive-green sweater with epaulettes. Shoba was in a pink and gold squared silk sari, wore elaborate toe rings and her toe- and fingernails had been freshly painted a brilliantly pink. She would not have looked out of place in the fashionable circles of Bombay or Delhi. Shiv Narayan had a motorbike. On his way to work, he turned down the avenue leading to the jail and dropped me off at the offices in front of the massive jail door.

I asked to see the superintendent and was ushered into his room and told to wait. He had a large office, complete with carpet and a huge wooden desk with every imaginable acces- sory – telephones, blotters, brass bells – all neatly arranged. I contemplated these for over an hour before being summoned to meet him on the veranda of his house opposite.

The jail superintendent was fat, with a very short neck. His stumpy fingers were festooned with heavy gold rings set with multiple precious stones. He did not look pleasant. When I asked if I could visit Phoolan, he said that the Inspector- General had instructed that all applications must be referred to the Home Secretary in the Madhya Pradesh capital, Bhopal. He insisted that it was more than his job was worth to let me meet her. I got the impression that this was probably true and that he was not looking for a bribe. However, I was not very good at that sort of thing. I asked about the postal orders for £100 that I had sent to Phoolan. He told me that he had referred the matter to the Home Secretary in Bhopal but received no response. He gave me an address to write to.

As I left, I took a couple of surreptitious photos of the Victorian-Gothic jail. Some children thought I was photographing them and waved their cricket bats. I walked back to the main road and took an auto-rickshaw into town. It had been a depressing meeting. Even if I travelled to Bhopal, it seemed unlikely that the authorities there would let me see Phoolan – certainly not in a hurry – and I was leaving India at the end of the week.

In the evening, Shiv Narayan arrived at my hotel with two male friends and a man to translate. He seemed remarkably uninterested in who I was and why I was there. I had the impression that he found the whole Phoolan business an embarrassment for a bright young policeman. He told me that the three acres of agricultural land Phoolan had received as part of the surrender deal for 'resettlement' on her release were completely barren and worthless. He thought, however, that she would be fairly safe if she were freed. Not only had he acquired a gun for himself but he had also purchased one for her, in her own name. This he had managed to do easily enough, he told me to my astonishment, as since she had never been through the courts she had no formal criminal record.

We discussed the 'missing' £100. He told me that I should address any valuables for Phoolan care of himself. When I asked if I could send anything useful for her, he said that radios, which I had suggested, were forbidden but that she would like a tiny camera. I promised to send him one, for him to smuggle in to her. I thought this rather odd. Meanwhile, I gave him the picture of the goddess Vindhyavasini Devi that I had brought from the temple near Mirzapur. He promised to give it to Phoolan.

As Shiv Narayan left, I asked him to give Phoolan my best wishes and to tell her to keep out of politics and to follow Kamini Jaiswal's advice. I also asked him if I could meet the rest of the family. They might, I thought, be more forthcoming. He was not keen and fobbed me off.

I supposed that I had made some progress but, all in all, I was very disappointed. I had really wanted to meet Phoolan face to face.

I spent the next two days looking around Gwalior. The smaller streets were like most in India, with the buildings that housed offices and shops looking somewhat dilapidated. Paintwork was peeling and structural repairs half-finished. Everywhere there were festoons of unsafe-looking electric cables that led to antique fuse boxes. Pedestrians were a low priority and pavements were either non-existent or potholed. Surprisingly, though, the central square was attractive and well maintained. It had flower gardens and palm trees. Even more surprising, for such colonial relics had usually been removed after independence, it was still called George V Square and there was an impressive statue of that king and emperor. Nevertheless, the pavements had been taken over by hawkers of cheap clothes and foodstuffs. One seller was doing brisk business selling potions for 'sexual problems' and 'magical' charms. I bought an extraordinary carving made from a tree root. It was fashioned into the shape of two embracing spirits, complete with eyes and weird growths coming out of their mouths.

I visited the impressive palace of the Maharaja. In a vast central room there was a dining table that could seat a huge number of guests. It was fitted with a model-railway system to circulate port and cigars. It was said that the Maharaja would accelerate it past guests he did not greatly like. There were photographs of the massive chandelier that hung from the ceiling that showed its hook being tested for strength by suspending an elephant from it. On the floor was the 'biggest carpet in the world'. It had been woven by the inmates of Gwalior Jail.

I ate at the Indian Coffee House. India was a major producer of coffee but obtaining good coffee was extremely difficult. Usually you were offered 'real Nescafé' or, even worse, coffee laced with chicory. Most towns, however, had Indian Coffee Houses. They were run by the coffee farmers' cooperatives and served excellent coffee and good food. Supposedly they were the haunts of intellectuals and so there were newspapers. I read that violence had again erupted in Bombay. The latest figure was a hundred and seventy-seven dead. Those that could were fleeing the city. There were predictions that the violence would once again spread across India so I was glad that I was almost at the end of my visit.

*

On Wednesday evening I returned to Delhi. I rang Kamini Jaiswal to tell her what had happened in Gwalior. She was sympathetic and we promised to keep in touch. I spent Thursday and Friday sightseeing and buying gifts. I also visited the British Council to float the idea of them financing me to run a book and archive conservation programme. I would have liked to live in India for a year or two. They were quite keen but said that the Indian authorities did not give much priority to conservation, so I did not think it would happen. It was another disappointment.

On 16 January, I arrived at Delhi airport for the early morning flight back to London, via Moscow. We eventually departed at 11 a.m. the next day. I landed at Heathrow extremely tired but already planning to return to India on my next annual leave. There were a lot of places I wanted to visit. Maybe, I thought, Phoolan would by then have been released. At the very least, I might be able to meet her inside the jail.

*

On my return to London, I wrote to Phoolan to say how disappointed I was not to have met her. I told her that I thought the Supreme Court would order her release fairly soon, and urged her to keep silent and let Kamini Jaiswal speak on her behalf. Also, I told her that I had written to the Home Department in Bhopal asking them to either give her the £100 or return the postal orders to me. I pointed out that they would expire on 14 February, so if they were not cashed by then, I could re-send the money to someone she trusted. I asked her to let me know. I mentioned that I was sending 'some present' to Shiv Narayan for her.

With the letter I enclosed a photograph of the flowers floating down the River Ganges. I also bought a Fuji camera for £25 and sent it off to Shiv Narayan for Phoolan. I hoped that he was not taking me for a ride.

In the middle of February a letter from Phoolan arrived, which Ajit translated.

Letter from Gwalior Jail, dated 4 February 1993:

Respected Brother,

My respectful greetings to you. I am well by the grace of God and pray for you and your family's well being. I received your letter today and came to know that you are sending 'some present', which I know nothing about. I ask you not to send anything. Do not send anything at my brother's or my family's request. If you sent anything write to me, as my family don't tell me anything. They are all selfish in this respect and are out to swindle everyone by using my name.

I have not received 'that money', so ask for it back. You can then send it to Phoolan Devi, daughter of Devidin, account no. 12390, passbook no 77/362, at the Bank of Maharashtra. Do let me know what my family asked from you. I really feel it when my family use my name to ask people for things.

I am going to Uttar Pradesh. My advocate doesn't seem to be doing anything and I don't know what is happening. I felt really sad that you came to India and we could not meet.

I am giving you Mala Sen's address. She wrote a book about me and is making a film too. Please tell her Phoolan wants to see her and that what was agreed on must be adhered to, otherwise I will seek help in the courts. Please see her and tell her she must come to India immediately to sort out the money. The work on the film has already begun. If Mala Sen doesn't come, I'll file a writ in the High Court to stop the film about me being made.

Please do write to me regarding the present my family has asked from you. Do not send anything.

My regards to you and your family, my love to the children, and my greetings to your friends.

Your Sister,
Phoolan Devi

This was the first that I had heard about Phoolan and a film. I assumed that it would be a documentary. I wondered why Phoolan needed to use me as an intermediary but, nevertheless, was pleased to see that she valued my judgement and trusted me to act for her. It would be a good opportunity to meet Mala Sen, whose book I admired, and who might be a useful source of information about Phoolan.

Mala Sen's address in London was inserted in English. Coincidentally, that day there was an article in the *Guardian* by Mala Sen headed 'A Bandit Queen Betrayed'. She wrote that a decision from the Supreme Court was expected that week – 'Her prospects remain grim whatever the outcome: if she is extradited to Uttar Pradesh, she believes she will be hanged; even if released, she will live as a fugitive; or, more likely, the Supreme Court will stall and she will remain in jail.'

Letter to Mala Sen, dated 16 February 1993:

Dear Mala Sen,

I have just had a letter from Phoolan Devi, who has asked me
to contact you about some matters.

Her letter is somewhat confused (and maybe a little paranoid!) and I should like to talk to you, so that I can sensibly
reassure her, and pass on what she has written.

Since starting my correspondence with Phoolan Devi, I
have read your book (and your latest piece in the *Guardian*)
and much appreciate what you have done to help her cause.

Also, I met Kamini Jaiswal in Delhi in mid-January, and she
has asked that, if I was in touch with you, I mention that she
has been unable to contact you and that she needed to clarify
some details of the Phoolan Devi case with you.

I am away in Canterbury during the week, but am back at
the address above at weekends, and would be very grateful if
you could ring me.

Yours sincerely,
Roy Moxham

Mala Sen phoned and invited me to Sunday lunch at her flat
in Clapham. I showed her Phoolan's letter and she became
extremely upset that Phoolan was so suspicious of her. She
said that she had been trying to help Phoolan for the last eight
years and that she did not sleep for worry. Although she was an
attractive woman in her forties, she looked very strained.

Mala showed me a copy of a letter from the film company to
Phoolan's bank, which enclosed a money order for 200,000
rupees (c. £4,000). I gathered that the film was being made by
Channel 4, the TV company, but would be a full-length film for
cinema. Mala was going to India the next week to work on a
new project in Rajasthan. She said that she might or might not
meet Phoolan in Gwalior since she felt that Phoolan was very

ungrateful for what she had done for her. Mala was instrumental in getting Kamini Jaiswal to represent Phoolan. She emphasised what a good lawyer Kamini was and how lucky Phoolan was to have her. I tried to pour oil on the waters by pointing out that Phoolan was bound to be paranoid after so many years in prison. I promised to write a sharp letter to her.

Mala talked at length and it was 4 p.m. by the time we had lunch. It was a very useful meeting. I hoped she and Phoolan could become friends again.

I wrote to Phoolan. I told her that I had already despatched a cheap camera to Shiv Narayan. I told her about my meeting with Mala Sen and of seeing the letter to the bank. I also informed her that Mala Sen was coming to India and perhaps travelling to Gwalior but that she was very upset. I urged her to try and repair their friendship.

I now come to the most important thing in this letter – your lawyer. I wrote to you about his matter before, but you make no mention of this in your letter, so I will tell you again. Your case is in the Supreme Court and you must have a good Supreme Court lawyer, or you will never be free. Kamini Jaiswal is just such a lawyer. Normally such a lawyer would cost you many lakhs [one lakh = 100,000 rupees]. She is representing you without taking a fee, and you should take her advice and treat her with great respect. If she becomes upset with you, and refuses to continue with your case, you will never get such a good lawyer again. I know you find the delays frustrating, but it is not her fault, and it is the way the courts operate in these important cases. This is a very big case and you must have a first-class lawyer. Some local lawyers will promise you your freedom and take your money, but do nothing. Small lawyers may seem very clever to uneducated people, but in the Supreme Court they are laughed at. Keep Kamini Jaiswal as your only lawyer, and do what she advises.

I hope you do not find this letter too outspoken. I know it is difficult for you there in jail, where you cannot get proper information, and where people take advantage of your lack of education. I am very sorry that we could not meet. However, I write what I honestly believe will help you.

I sent Mala Sen a copy. I felt rather out of my depth, so hoped I had done what was for the best. Although I only had a limited knowledge of India, I was certain that Kamini Jaiswal was the best lawyer that Phoolan could possibly have. I felt that, even at the risk of appearing overbearing, it was important to communicate this firmly to Phoolan. Moreover, I feared that if Phoolan carried out her expressed intention to leave Gwalior, and agreed to be extradited to Uttar Pradesh, she was probably going to die – she would either be sentenced to death by the judiciary or be murdered by the police. A few days later, I telephoned Mala Sen to thank her for her hospitality. She was pleased with my letter and said that she would write to me from India.

Later, I reflected on how my relationship with Phoolan had gradually been transformed. I had moved from asking her if I could help to telling her what would be best. I might have obtained some of the confidence to do this from experiences in my colonial past. When only twenty-one I had found myself running a tea estate with over five hundred workers. I had been startled to be asked by the workers to adjudicate in cases among them of assault or adultery. When I protested that these were matters for the police or a magistrate, my objections were brushed aside. 'Previous *bwanas* settled these matters,' I was told, 'it's much more convenient for us than if we have to travel a long distance and then have to wait ages for justice. If any of us objects to your judgement we can always pursue the matter elsewhere.'

Traditionally, disputes were settled with money, as in a civil case, which made things easier for me. I soon found myself arbitrating in dozens of cases and awarding 'damages' to whomever

I decided was the aggrieved party. This system came to a halt with the end of colonialism and the arrival of independence, but I was left with a certain confidence in my ability to arbitrate.

*

Early in March, I wrote to the post office to reclaim the uncashed postal orders. A week later, a letter arrived from Phoolan. Sharada, an Indian student I had become friendly with, translated it for me.

Letter from Gwalior Jail, dated 3 March 1993:

Victory to Goddess Durga

Respected Mr Roy,

Greetings from Phoolan to my brother. I am well and hope that all is well with you and your family. I am sorry for this late reply, which is due to ill health. Please tell Mala Sen that I am not angry with her. From the day that they started shooting the film lots of people have been telling me that I will not be released from jail and probably hanged. So, respected brother, I became nervous and apprehensive. They told me that Mala Sen has trapped me and that I would not be released. I have been unable to sleep or eat properly. I became very agitated and wrote all sorts of things that I regret. I respect Mala Sen – she is like an elder sister to me. But Mr Bedi [the film's producer] is making a fool of me and is not paying me anything.

In anger I also wrote to Kamini Jaiswal that as I was going to die here, I might as well go to Uttar Pradesh and die there. Brother I did it because stories from people here made me afraid. Respected brother, you are right when you say I am illiterate and that I am taken in by whatever I am told by whoever says it. I have been betrayed many times, yet I trust everyone. From now on I will not listen to those people and will do as Kamini Jaiswal suggests. Please write to her and ask her to file a petition for my release as soon as possible. I will not ask any other lawyer to do anything. Brother, you are wise and experienced, so keep giving me your advice. I will do whatever you tell me to do.

The £100 you sent me is still lying here in Gwalior Jail and I have not been given it. Ask for your money back. Send it to my bank account as in my previous letter and I will give it to Kamini Jaiswal.

Shiv Narayan told me that he asked you for a camera. Indians are very dishonest. When it comes to asking for favours they all become my relatives and well-wishers.

I enclose a letter for Mala Sen. Please give it to her and assure her that I am not angry with her. Do write to Kamini Jaiswal and ask her to do whatever she thinks should be done.

I also enclose some coloured powder for the festival of Holi – do put it on your forehead and on those of your dear ones. Especially on that of your wife. Dear sister-in-law, are you annoyed with me that you have never sent your greetings? I send my greetings to you. Do put this powder on my respected brother and all the children.

I am ending my letter now. If I am released alive, then I will surely meet you and sister-in-law, and all your children and friends. If I die, then in my next birth. If there were good people like you in India then poor helpless women like me would not be destroyed. Brother, when you came to India we could not meet each other. I was really sad and I started cursing God. But what could I do, such are my misfortunes?

Brother, do forgive the mistakes in this letter and reply soon.

Your Sister,
Phoolan Devi

I wrote to Kamini Jaiswal in Delhi, enclosing a copy of my letter to Phoolan – *I know you have had a thankless task defending her, but hope she will now be more reasonable. I shall be writing to her regularly, to exhort her to stay with you and be co-operative.*

I also enclosed, and asked her to forward to Mala Sen, the letter that Phoolan had written to Mala. I had asked Sharada, a little guiltily, to look through that letter too. Phoolan had written that she had had trouble with her eyes and that the prison warders wanted 50,000 rupees – from the film money – before they would allow her to see a doctor. I asked Kamini to try and get treatment to Phoolan.

I also sent a letter to Phoolan:

> I have written to Kamini Jaiswal telling her to proceed with your case as fast as she can. I explained how you had been confused, and promised her you would be respectful to her, and take her advice. Believe me, this is a very wise thing for you to have done. I am sure she will manage to free you.

I told her that I had forwarded her letter to Mala Sen and that I was glad that she wanted the two of them to be reconciled.

I thanked her for the Holi pigment and explained my family situation – *I have to tell you that although I am not properly married, my girlfriend sends her good wishes to you as well. Not being married or having children may seem strange to you in India, but here in London it is quite usual.* I wondered what she would think of that. My giving the impression that I had a regular girlfriend was playing with the truth. Although over the years I had had a variety of girlfriends, I had no intention of adding Phoolan to the list. I thought this white lie would be the best way to allay any idea that Phoolan might have that my interest in her was other than platonic.

I told her that I was still trying to have the postal orders refunded. I also put a rather positive gloss on her future, feeling it might save her from depression:

> I now come to the most important thing in this letter. You must stop thinking you will be hanged. There is no chance of

that. I spoke frankly to Kamini Jaiswal, who is very experienced in these cases, and she is absolutely sure they will never hang you. The case is now too old. If they had wanted you dead they would have done it long ago. I have spoken to many other educated Indians, and they all agree that there is absolutely no possibility that you will be hanged. The courts never allow hanging of people, even if they are guilty, after such a long time waiting in prison.

I really think you may be released this year. However, the courts move very slowly, and it is possible it may take a bit longer. However, I repeat, there is no chance of you being hanged in Madhya Pradesh, Uttar Pradesh, or anywhere else. You can be sure of that.

Spring is here in England, and the flowers are all in bloom. I hope you will soon be out of prison, and able to see flowers for yourself.

A couple of days later a letter, which must have crossed mine, arrived from Phoolan.

Letter from Gwalior Jail, dated 14 April 1993:

Victory to Goddess Durga

Respected Mr Roy Moxham, greetings from Phoolan. I was very happy to read your letter. Mala is in India. You told me to keep on good terms with Kamini Jaiswal and I shall heed your advice. She is a good lawyer who is handling my case well. The case is in court on the 16th and 17th. They should decide, Jesus willing, over the next two to four months whether to free me. Brother, please pray to God Jesus for my early release.

I felt sad when I read your letter that you did not get married at the right time and have children, who are the only support in old age. Brother, you are really like me – I never married and had children. Still I am happy you have a girlfriend and consider her my sister-in-law. Give her my greetings and thanks. Brother, if with your good wishes I am freed, I will praise you, do whatever I can for you and see that you are not alone. Brother, I have gone through a lot in my life and if I take care of you it will bring me inner happiness.

The officials have not given me the camera. You should ask for it back. They are all crooked and do not give us our gifts even after we have signed for them. I give the postman 10 or 20 rupees to give me some letters direct.

My health is somewhat better now. A doctor came from outside to treat me. Brother you also take care of yourself. You are very understanding so please excuse any mistakes in this letter.

My elder sister Rukhmani's son, Mathura Prasad, is being married. The Tika ceremony [when the bride's family come with gifts for the groom's family] is on 4th May. I know you cannot come as London is so far away but, nevertheless, I invite you. I send greetings to your girlfriend too and invite her. I may get permission to attend. My young brother, Shiv Narayan, thinks you are a really good person and sends you his greetings.

I hope you have asked for your money back. Otherwise, the jail officials will swallow it. Let me know.

Brother, the first thing I shall do when I am released from jail is try to meet you. If I am released I will above all try to meet you.

Your sister,
Phoolan Devi

I sent a reply and told her I was still chasing up the postal order refund. I enclosed a copy of the certificate of posting I received when I despatched the camera to Shiv Narayan. I wrote that if he did not receive it he should send me an official letter to make a claim here. I warned her that a false declaration would result in prosecution.

You must not feel too sad that I am not properly married and do not have children. I have a good girlfriend (who sends her greetings to you) and two younger brothers and five nephews and nieces. Also, things are very different here in England, because the government gives everyone a pension when they are old.

My mother is still alive and in good health. She sends the enclosed photo of herself, and her best wishes for your early release written on the back.

I now come to an important matter. If you are released on parole, until your case is finally decided you should be very quiet when you are outside the prison. You will be tempted to say hard things about those who have kept you captive for so long. However, they are more likely to allow you your freedom if they think you will keep quiet. Also you have made many enemies in the past, and it will be better for you if you do not goad them into revenge. Keep quiet until your freedom is permanent.

Most of all, keep out of politics. Everywhere in the world politicians are a nasty lot. They will try to use you, then sacrifice you when it is to their advantage. Do not trust them. Keep to your family, and to your old and reliable friends.

My best wishes to you. I shall probably come to India next year. By then, I am sure you will be free, and that we shall finally meet each other. You may have a few setbacks, but try not to worry too much. Nothing very bad will happen to you now.

For six weeks I waited anxiously for a reply. As I walked to work in the archive from my home in the precincts of Canterbury Cathedral, I would make my way along the cloister. Somehow, the enclosed quadrangle triggered off thoughts of Phoolan in her prison yard. Perhaps it was an echo of that bleak picture by Gustave Doré of prisoners exercising. It was a relief to finally receive a letter, although it was not encouraging about her health.

Letter from Gwalior Jail, dated 13 June 1993:

Victory to Goddess Durga

Greetings from Phoolan to respected brother Roy Moxham,

I hope you and your family are well. I am now a little better. Brother, please do not be angry that I have not replied sooner. I had stomach ache and was vomiting blood. I was in Kamla Raja Hospital for ten or fifteen days and even now my health is not good. As soon as I felt a bit better I sat down and dictated this letter. Please write to Mala Sen and Kamini Jaiswal to tell them I am ill and to seek my earliest possible release.

I have received the camera from Shiv Narayan. Please do not mention this in your letters. Ask for your £100 back and send it to my account.

Please give my special good wishes to your mother. I look at her photograph every day and feel happy. When I am released I will come to London to see you and your mother. Brother, you are right when you say that the politicians here are making me a scapegoat. Now I say to everybody who comes to meet me – 'First get me released, then I will seek election.' Please write to Kamini Jaiswal about my release, which I need to get proper medical treatment. The jail officials are all after money – and from where do I get this bribe money? I pray to God to let me die rather than live this sort of life.

Brother, please keep writing to me. Here in India it is extremely hot, which is why I had blood in my vomit. Please write to Kamini Jaiswal urging her to get me released as soon as possible – otherwise I may die here. I am unwell and the jailers treat me very badly. Do not worry – now I will not be taken in by politicians' sweet-talk. I understand this much – that I am in jail and none of these people help me. If I am released I will go somewhere and start an independent life.

Please excuse any mistakes in this letter. My best respects to you and your mother. May god Jesus take care of you. My best regards to your girlfriend, and my love to all my nephews and nieces. Shiv Narayan and his wife send their good wishes. I would really like to meet you – you are a dear member of my family to me and I really respect you. Please ask Mala Sen to let me know whether she is still in India. My sister's son's wedding went off well. Mathura and his bride send warm wishes to you.

Phoolan Devi

I found this letter incredibly moving. It kept resurfacing in my memory to make me sad. I wrote to Kamini Jaiswal. I enclosed a copy of Phoolan's letter, mentioned her deteriorating health, and asked if this might expedite her release.

I wrote back to Phoolan.

I told her that I had written to Kamini Jaiswal to urge her early release.

Also I have spoken to my brother John about your illness. He is a very important doctor here, and a professor of medicine at London University. Of course, he can only guess what is wrong, as he has not seen you. However, he thinks that it is most likely you have an ulcer. He advises you as follows (even if the trouble is something other than an ulcer, this will not harm you) –

1. Try and eat food without much spice, especially avoid red chilli peppers.
2. Drink a little milk as often as you can, especially before you eat.
3. Do not smoke tobacco.
4. Take anti-acid indigestion tablets (magnesium). These are easily obtained from any chemist, and are not expensive. You should take them several times a day, following the instructions on the packet.

I know this will be difficult for you, but even if your health is a bit better you should follow his advice for a few months.

Then you will fully recover. Of course, if the prison doctor gives you proper anti-ulcer tablets, you will not need the extra ones. But follow the other recommendations.

I have just been visiting the little town where I was born, to see my mother. She was glad you liked her photo and sends her greetings to you. Also my girlfriend, family and other friends send their good wishes.

I do hope you are feeling a bit better. You must not despair, as I am confident you will soon be released. The courts are slow, but eventually they will agree to your lawyer's request. I am sure we shall meet – perhaps next year – and very much look forward to that.

Remember to keep out of politics, and stick carefully to the advice of Kamini Jaiswal.

In July I finally received a refund from the Post Office. I went to the State Bank of India and purchased a draft for £100. Actually, it was slightly more, as I made it up to 5,001 rupees. The extra rupee, I had been told, was considered lucky in India. I noticed the bank staff looking strangely at me when they saw the draft was made out to Phoolan Devi. However, no one said anything. I sent off the draft to the Bank of Maharashtra, Gwalior. Come the end of August I had received no communication from Phoolan. I wrote to her to ask if she had received my letter and whether she was following John's medical advice. I also told her that I had sent off the draft for 5,001 rupees. I asked for any news about her release. I told her that I was planning my birthday party and enclosed a postcard of Piccadilly Circus.

By the end of September I had still heard nothing and was worried. However, at the beginning of October a letter arrived. It was not good news.

Letter from Gwalior Jail, undated but postmarked 25 September 1993:

Hail Durga Ma

Greetings from sister Phoolan to respected brother Roy Moxham,

I am sending you lots and lots of good wishes for your birthday. I pray to the goddess Durga for your long life and that even the remaining years of my life be given to you.

Brother, I am ill. I have been diagnosed with two stomach tumours – one near the liver and the other near the kidneys. I cannot eat or digest properly and I have a problem with my bowels. I have become very weak. I cannot eat or drink properly or move about, and have to keep lying down all day. The court instructed that I should be operated upon, but some people have advised me not to have this, as it would stop my release. Brother, I have already had two operations and I don't understand why tumours develop again and again. The doctors do not give me any medication but say I should have the operation. I follow your advice and drink fresh milk. Brother, pray for my early release so that I can meet my brother and his mother. If not, I pray for my death, which would be better than a life like this.

Brother, I am not a criminal such as has been made out. In reality, I haven't committed any crime nor committed any murder with these hands. I did not wish to become a dacoit. They kidnapped me from my home, yet I have been portrayed as a dacoit and a criminal – why? Those who became dacoits by their own free will have been released. Why this injustice to me? Those who were bigger criminals were left untouched by the government. They deserved to be punished, but were not punished.

Brother, please reply soon. I don't know what is happening with my court case. Please accept my warm wishes and I remember all of you. My warmest greetings to my brother and mother and my love to the children. Whenever I see the photograph of your mother I feel better. I don't know whether

God will let us meet. Please give my respectful greetings to your girlfriend and the person who translates my letters for you. Brother, please reply soon.

Your sister,
Phoolan Devi

I spoke with my brother, then quickly replied:

Greetings. I hope you are not feeling too ill and that you are managing to eat better.

I was sad to get your letter and learn that you have been so sick. I have discussed everything with my brother John, the doctor. He says you must have the operation immediately.

If you leave the operation then the tumours will multiply and they will spread. It is very important that you have the operation right away. Of course, all of us are frightened by operations. I tell you frankly, I would be frightened if it were me. But I would definitely have the operation. There is no effective medicine for a tumour. You must have it cut out straight away.

Do not bother about the operation delaying your release. I do not think it will make any difference to when they release you.

I shall try and telephone your lawyer and find out the latest situation. It is difficult from here. When I find out I will write to you again. I am not delaying sending this letter, as I wanted to tell you to have the operation urgently.

I completely agree with what you say in your letter. It is very unfair that you, who only became a dacoit because you were kidnapped, should suffer the most. I think it is because you are a woman, and because your case is so well known.

However, do not despair. Even here in England these big cases move slowly. They will have to release you soon. Your case is so old that they cannot bring new charges. All the old charges are dismissed. Now that you have a good lawyer in the Supreme Court, they will have to let you go soon. Do what Kamini Jaiswal advises and do not lose hope. I am planning to come to India early in 1994. I expect to be able to visit you, as you will be free.

Best wishes from my mother, my family, my girlfriend, and all my other friends. My friend, Sharada, who translated your letter, sends her good wishes too.

Have the operation now. I shall think of you.

Later in October, I finally managed to get through on the phone to Kamini Jaiswal in Delhi. Phoolan had been transferred to Tihar Jail in Delhi so that she could have the operation. By order of the court, this was to be done at the prestigious All India Institute of Medical Sciences. However, Phoolan was frustrating Kamini by delaying things. I told her that I would write to Phoolan again. I thought that perhaps she had not received my last letter, which I had sent to Gwalior.

Kamini told me that Phoolan's case was due in court again in November. She thought Phoolan would be released before I went to India in February. This was very good news. It was the first time she had made such a confident assertion. It made me feel much more hopeful about Phoolan's future – providing her health improved.

I wrote to Phoolan at Tihar Jail, enclosing a copy of the letter I had written to her in Gwalior, which urged her to have the operation.

You should not worry that having the operation will delay your release. I have asked Kamini Jaiswal about this. She says it will make no difference at all. She went to a lot of trouble to get an order from the Supreme Court for you to have medical treatment. The court have arranged for you to see very good doctors. These are much better doctors than you would find in Gwalior. You should follow their advice and have the operation.

I also spoke to Kamini Jaiswal about your application for release. She tells me the case is progressing well. The

Supreme Court will be hearing the matter again next month.
She is confident that when I come to India in February you will
be free. So do not despair. You have an excellent lawyer. Do
what she tells you, and you will soon be released.

As 1993 came to an end, I became worried again. I had heard
nothing from Phoolan since September. I thought that maybe
my letters did not reach her in the Delhi jail, or that maybe she
could not send replies. Or, worse, maybe she was too ill.

Often, as I concentrated on my work, Phoolan would enter
my mind. The conservation that I was carrying out at
Canterbury was complicated. There had been a fire in the
cathedral's Audit House in 1670. This had set fire to the roof.
Some records had been irretrievably burnt and others had been
severely damaged by the water used to put out the fire and the
rain that had come in through the roof. Many of the dampened
documents went mouldy. A century later piles of these archives
still remained on the floor as they disintegrated. My job was to
salvage whatever was left of the most important records and
put them into a state where they could be safely handled.

The work was demanding. There was much delicate cleaning to be done. The acid induced by the mould often had to
be neutralised by immersing the documents in an alkaline
solution. This was tricky, since they were written in inks that
might run. Leaves with ragged edges had to be inlaid into new
paper or vellum and then bound up. Month after month, I
stood at my bench desperately concentrating. Even so, I would
suddenly realise that I was also worrying about Phoolan.

I wrote to her yet again, reiterating my previous advice. I told
her that I would be coming to India at the end of February for
five weeks. I hoped, I said, that then she would be free and that
we would meet. I sent her a Christmas card with a picture of a
snowman and gave her a brief description of our winter and of
Christmas. I imagined that she had never seen snow.

3
Freedom?

'Trust in the Goddess Durga – she will look after you.'

AT THE beginning of 1994, I bought a ticket for India – leaving on 27 February and returning on 10 April. Uppermost in my mind was the desire to finally meet Phoolan, either in jail, or, more hopefully, free. I had still heard nothing from her. I was not, however, expecting too much from a meeting. I had drawn up a comprehensive itinerary of places around India that I wanted to visit and expected that this would occupy most of my time.

In the middle of January, I received a registered letter, dated 27 December, from the Superintendent of Gwalior Jail enclosing the expired postal orders. It was copied to: 'The Superintendent, Tihar Jail, New Delhi with the request to inform the contents to Phoolan Devi, surrendered dacoit, confined to Tihar Jail.' So, it seemed that Phoolan was still in Delhi.

On 21 January there was a paragraph in the *Guardian* from Reuters saying that the new Chief Minister of Uttar Pradesh had announced the previous day that he would drop all charges against Phoolan. It was, however, not clear whether this would result in her release.

Next day, I received a New Year's card from Shiv Narayan with his good wishes for 1994. There was a brief message to say that Phoolan was in Tihar Jail. I thought it was good of him to write.

At the beginning of February, there was a lengthy article in the *Independent* by Tim McGirk. He thought that Phoolan would probably be free within a month – 'Her enemies are the state's powerful high-caste Thakurs, the landowners, who wish her dead . . . Her Robin Hood-like notoriety is a sure vote-puller among Uttar Pradesh's lower castes, which view her as a champion of the oppressed. Uttar Pradesh, India's most populous state, is controlled by a coalition of socialists and the outcaste Untouchables. For them she is a heroine, a wronged woman who dared fight back against the ruling classes.'

I realised that I would to have to be very careful about what I did, and said, when I went to India.

I wrote to Phoolan to tell her that I would arrive in India on the 28th, and that I would contact Kamini Jaiswal to find out what was happening.

> It is good news that all the charges in Uttar Pradesh have been dropped. Also that the Chief Minister is saying that you have suffered enough. I hope the Central Government and the courts will take his advice. The English newspapers say that you will be released very soon.
>
> When you are released, you must be very careful. It will be better if you keep very quiet for a while. The relatives of those who were killed may try and seek revenge if you say too much. Remember also, you have been in jail for many years. It will be strange for you to be free. It will be best for your health to be quiet for a while. Go and stay with your relatives and old friends until you see how things are. Do not say too much to the press and television. Above all, keep out of politics. After six months of freedom, you will be clear in your mind, and then you can decide what to do.

On Saturday 19 February my friend Tamara phoned to say that she had just heard on the 9 a.m. BBC news that Phoolan had been released. Even though the newspapers had prepared me for this, I was stunned. It was hard for me to take in.

I rapidly searched that morning's *Guardian*. I found a report that on the previous day the Supreme Court had ordered her release on parole, on condition that she posted a bond before a magistrate. Her release was on parole because the courts in Uttar Pradesh had yet to confirm the government's decision to drop the charges. The Supreme Court had also ordered that she receive police protection.

I still could not quite believe that she was free. However, when I tuned into the BBC World Service later that morning they had an eyewitness account. The reporter described how Phoolan had signed the release paper with her thumbprint. Kamini Jaiswal then spoke briefly to say that Phoolan was to stay in the care of an uncle in Delhi. As I was flying into Delhi and had contact details for Kamini Jaiswal, this was perfect for me.

I had hardly dared hope this would happen. It looked as though we would meet at last. But, I wondered, would we have enough in common to relate to each other?

Various friends phoned, including Edward, whose Worcester branch of Amnesty International had adopted Phoolan. I was not sure whether any of our efforts had helped secure her release, but at least we had probably cheered her up when she was so low. In the evening Sharada came round with a friend and they took me out for a celebratory meal.

There were articles about Phoolan in the *Independent on Sunday* and in the *Sunday Times*. They both reported that several thousand cheering supporters greeted her as she came from the court. The *Independent* article was headlined 'Bandit Queen broken by Jail' and said that she looked frail and ill. It also mentioned that she needed an operation to remove a tumour. 'Asked what she would do now, she replied: "Whatever God wills." ' However, the *Sunday Times* article said that she intended to spend the rest of her life as an ascetic wandering the banks of the River Chambal singing holy songs.

A week after Phoolan's release I dropped into the Indian restaurant to say goodbye before I flew to India the following day. It was a good job I did. To Ajit's great amusement, the Hindi phrase I had been practising for 'elder sister' I was mispronouncing so that it meant 'evil sister'.

I was still trying not to expect too much from a meeting with Phoolan. I knew that lots of people who got themselves into trouble deserved help, but that did not necessarily mean they were very pleasant. There would be a language problem too. I expected that probably I would meet her just briefly and then go off on my travels. Nevertheless, I was excited.

*

It was a good flight to Delhi. I arrived on schedule at 5.15 a.m., then took a bus to Connaught Place. When I hailed a rickshaw to go on to Paharganj, the driver said – 'Sorry, that area is closed down because of Hindu and Muslim fighting. I can find you a place near here.' Suspecting I was being conned, I told him that, if necessary, I'd walk. He contemptuously handed me over to another driver. Actually, when we arrived at Paharganj, the problem was that most hotels were full. I trekked all over and eventually found an unpleasant room – dirty and with no bathroom. It was all rather depressing. However, I was tired, so I took the room and was soon asleep.

I woke at 1 p.m. I felt as if drugged but forced myself to go for lunch. Being the end of February, it was much hotter outside than on my previous visit. I trudged through the crowded bazaar to secure a better room at another hotel.

I rang Kamini Jaiswal at 6 p.m. 'Why don't you come over?' she said. 'Phoolan is probably coming too.' When I arrived, Kamini was in the middle of a consultation. However, she ordered coffee for me and we managed to chat intermittently. I gave her the chocolates that I had brought for her.

Kamini rang Phoolan and I could hear an excited voice. It seemed that Phoolan wanted me to go straight away and meet her. When Kamini explained to the auto-rickshaw driver where I was going, he nearly had a heart attack. It was a long journey. We had to cross New Delhi, then continue north for five miles to the other side of Old Delhi. When we reached the housing colony, which was situated in a moderately prosperous area, it was 9 p.m.

At Old Gupta Colony, the rickshaw turned towards what I thought was a small police station, but was a fortified residence. For defensive purposes, it was well situated at the end of a block. Outside, there was a tent protected by breezeblocks and a sandbagged sentry box. A dozen policemen had rifles or machine pistols. Wearing berets and khaki uniforms and mostly carrying old Lee-Enfield rifles, they looked like World War II soldiers. (Later, I found out these men were an addition to the Delhi police bodyguards, ordered by the Supreme Court, and had been sent to Delhi by the Chief Minister of Uttar Pradesh, Mulayam Singh.) I was searched very thoroughly by the Delhi police at the entrance and then stepped into the hallway. I was then interrogated by a superintendent of police. At first he was sceptical of my protestations that I was a friend of Phoolan's, but he finally let me past. Several of Phoolan's 'uncles' greeted me, two of them speaking fair English. We then went upstairs, where there were dozens of relatives and children. Shortly afterwards, escorted by a bodyguard with a sub-machine gun, Phoolan arrived.

Phoolan Devi was a much smaller woman than I had imagined. She must have been less than five feet tall. She was also very thin – not at all like in the photos taken at her surrender eleven years previously. It was difficult to imagine her carrying a heavy weapon. Prison had transformed her physique. Nevertheless, she looked amazingly well and happy, and delighted to see me.

Phoolan was wearing a simple pink sari, draped with a heavy maroon shawl, small gold earrings, glass bangles and silver rings on all the fingers of her right hand. Her intensely black hair straggled over her neck, and her face was continually lit up by a broad smile. Although she was supposedly thirty-two or more, she looked somewhat younger. The bodyguard had fair English. With him interpreting, we were soon exchanging rather stilted greetings and compliments. She was obviously very touched, and slightly bewildered, by my assistance.

'It was a great surprise to receive your letters,' she said. 'What made you write?'

'I don't know. I suppose that I felt that life had been very unfair to you and that I wanted to help.'

'I'm very grateful that you did. Your letters calmed me. Especially when I thought I would be hanged'

'That would never have happened.'

'Perhaps not. But the jail was taking away my life.'

'Well, now you are free!'

'Yes.' Her forehead wrinkled into a deep frown. 'But for how long? My cases are still before the courts. They might send me to jail again.'

'Trust in the Goddess Durga – she will look after you.'

'Yes.' A smile returned to her face. 'You are right. She is favouring me.'

We were disturbed by some artists who had arrived with a large painting of Phoolan. It was not a good likeness and looked more like an icon of a goddess. They were exhibiting at the annual art show, which opened in Delhi the following day, and wanted Phoolan to attend. She asked me for my opinion. I gathered that she had not been out of the house since her arrival over a week ago. She would have to venture out at some stage and maybe an art exhibition would be as innocuous a venue as any for her to test the waters. I suggested that she asked the police for their views and, if they were in favour, she should go.

Food arrived for me – presumably the others had eaten earlier. There were dishes of vegetables and chapattis. Phoolan sat with me as I ate and ladled out the food. When, at about 11 p.m., I said that I must go, everybody looked amazed. They had assumed that I would be staying the night. I had to promise Phoolan that I would leave my hotel next day and move in. I got back to Paharganj at midnight. It had been an extraordinary day.

*

I rose at 8 a.m. after a restless night as I wondered whether I was courting danger by moving into the Phoolan residence. I brushed aside my fears, checked out and set off for north Delhi. On the way, I bought Phoolan some flowers. This seemed an appropriate gift, as I had already noticed other bouquets around the house. Moreover her name, Phoolan Devi, meant 'goddess of flowers'. Phoolan seemed delighted and insisted on me re-presenting them to her for a photograph to be taken. Rather bizarrely, the roses remained wrapped in their cellophane. This was something I was often to see in India.

When I arrived, a crowded press photo-session was in progress. Phoolan was dressed in a brilliant red sari. Some representatives of the lower castes arrived to pay their respects. They too had their photographers.

Then we were off to Travancore Hall for the art exhibition. It was a bizarre scene. She and her entourage walked down a red carpet to applause and then climbed up onto the stage. Various people gave speeches in Hindi. Then Phoolan spoke. She seemed completely unfazed. There were dozens of photographers and TV cameras. Several people asked which news agency I was with. Phoolan was presented with a sculpture of the goddess Durga on a tiger and also with portraits by several artists of herself. Some of the onlookers seemed sympathetic;

others, obviously middle- or upper-class, were disdainful. An expensively dressed woman asked me who I was. When I said I was a friend of Phoolan, she gave me a look of total disbelief.

There was a sit-down tea. We were served English-style crustless cucumber sandwiches. I tried to keep in the background throughout the ceremonies but Phoolan summoned me to sit next to her. The press cameras homed in to capture the two of us sitting together. We went on a tour of the exhibition booths. It must have been a novel experience for Phoolan, but she looked at the paintings and talked to the artists as if to the manner born.

A huge crowd gathered to see Phoolan depart. When I tried to reach the front, an official elbowed me out of the way, shouting, 'She is leaving now.' Phoolan shouted back to him that I was staying with her and the crowd let me through. Just before I climbed into the car a European photographer whispered into my ear, 'It's a weird trip!'

Wherever we went, one of Phoolan's bodyguards from the Delhi police was with us, together with his sub-machine gun. When he waved it out of the car window, it had a salutatory effect on the congested traffic. He was always in the doorway as we ate or when guests arrived. Three bodyguards did shifts to give her twenty-four-hour cover. It was amazing how quickly I became used to them.

I found the policemen surprisingly pleasant. What I had read about police brutality in Uttar Pradesh had not led me to expect this. In India the police forces were structured along army lines with a separate, highly educated, officer class. It was almost impossible to progress, as in Britain, up through the ranks. The lower echelons were, in most parts of India, generally chosen solely for their physical fitness. Or that was the theory, because in practice they were often chosen after they had paid a bribe to secure the post. Once appointed they had to recover this money, and were not fussy about the methods they employed.

The Delhi police had a reputation of being much better than the average Indian police force. Those assigned to protection were the elite. They received extra pay and might secure exceptional promotion. The people they protected were mostly VIPs and it was in their interest to see that their bodyguards were well looked after. I met many and invariably found them congenial. They found it amusing when I told them of my time as a tea planter at the end of British rule in Africa. It had been a condition of my employment that I became an officer in the Colonial Police Reserve. My experiences then, at a time when Nyasaland was in a state of anxiety prior to independence, had given me many insights into police life. I had been issued with firearms, as the Delhi police were. I had acquired a good knowledge of pistols, rifles and even sub-machine guns during my colonial days. At times of tension I had often slept with a pistol by the side of my bed.

Phoolan and I had our evening meal. I was not very hungry but had to eat more than I wanted or appear rude. Phoolan was tired after the outing and lay resting. She must have found her first encounter with the outside world in over a decade traumatic, although she showed little outward sign of it.

We prepared for bed at 11 p.m. I had been placed in the 'study' on the ground floor. Actually, it was originally a shop, and had big plate-glass windows. I was a bit nervous sleeping behind so much glass. Earlier a police officer had taken me up onto the roof and enthused about what an excellent place it was for them to fire down on any attackers. A machine-gun was in place. Nevertheless, I counted myself lucky to get a room to myself, since there must have been at least twenty adults in the house, plus numerous children. Several men had bedded down in the hall outside my room. I had to pick my way between them when I got up in the night to visit the toilet.

*

Next morning I was woken up at 7.30 a.m. as some reporters arrived. I had slept quite well, although I had had to light a coil during the night to repel mosquitoes.

Dieter, a German photographer whom I had met the day before, arrived with an American woman who was doing an article for *Elle* magazine. His Indian girlfriend, Farah, came with him to do the translating. All were very sympathetic to Phoolan. I found the American, who had little experience of India, a bit banal. It was very useful for me, however, to hear Phoolan tell her life-story and have it translated. The most amazing part was when she described how in her early years with her own gang she had felt immune from capture. She said that as she slept on the ground, snakes would come and wake her up to warn of approaching danger, and that she would then escape. Subsequently, these snakes deserted her. It was then she realised that if she did not surrender, she would be caught.

Phoolan was extremely religious. She spent a lot of time in front of a shrine that she had assembled on a table against the wall in the living room. There were dozens of brilliantly coloured pictures of female goddesses – Kali, the goddess of time and destruction; Lakshmi, the bringer of wealth and happiness; Durga, the vanquisher of demons. Among the many pictures of Durga, I was pleased to see that there was the one from Mirzapur of Vindhyavasini Devi that I had given her in Gwalior Jail.

Phoolan also spent a good deal of time playing with the younger children. From the way she held them, it was clear that she would have liked some of her own. From what I had gathered about the assaults she had suffered, that did not seem likely.

Later in the day, I asked Phoolan about her medical condition and she showed me the doctors' reports. I saw that she did have a tumour but, fortunately, it was not malignant. This was a big relief to me. However, she did have ulcers, and there was no medicine left. I went with Rameshchander, one of several young married men in the family house, to get some made up at a pharmacy. I insisted they label the instructions in Hindi as most in the house had little knowledge of English. Even then, they would have given Phoolan the wrong dose had I not protested. Providing she obtained repeat prescriptions, and took the correct dose regularly, I thought she should be all right.

There was a continual stream of reporters and visitors all day. In the evening, Phoolan was involved in some intense discussions with remote relatives. I did not discover what this was about. My appetite had begun to return and I ate with Rameshchander. He worked for a bank, had excellent English, and was extremely helpful and intelligent. He was studying hard for an MBA, but his routine was being very much disrupted by the arrival of Phoolan, which the owner of the house, who had political ambitions, had engineered.

*

It was difficult for me to work out who was who in the fairly small house. I even failed to work out exactly how many inhab-itants there were. Including children, there were probably at least twenty-five. There was Phoolan's eldest sister, Rukhmani, and her teenage and very engaging son, Santosh. It was the house of Harphool Singh, an estate agent, his wife, Angroori Devi, their four married children and all of their children. I never managed to work out with certainty which were the Singhs' own offspring and which were the men or women they had married, but I did establish who was married to whom: Rameshchander to Risalo Devi, Hansraj to Maya Devi, Omprakesh to Sunita and Ashokumar to Sushila.

There were several other people staying at various times, including an extremely beautiful woman whom I never managed to place.

*

I awoke at seven thirty after a fitful night. I failed to get to the bathroom before the first visitors arrived. Phoolan had come down to the ground floor to talk to them. Space was limited, so she sat on my bed, with me still between the sheets, talking to them. The Hindi conversation washed over me as I silently urged them to go so that I could rush to the toilet.

Later, Maya Devi did me a special breakfast of toast with butter (her family normally never ate bread, only chapattis), which Phoolan shared with me. I taught her how to butter toast. After we had eaten, Phoolan took out a bottle of scent and rubbed some into my arms and neck. It took me aback. I hoped that it was just a normal Indian politeness and did not signify anything more intimate. I was determined to make it plain that I only had a brotherly, or perhaps avuncular, interest in her welfare, and thanked her rather formally.

A delegation from a remote village in Uttar Pradesh arrived. These men and women, mostly old, were obviously poor, with calloused hands and dressed in simple cotton clothes. Several of the women were widows, wearing the traditional white saris. They all tried to touch Phoolan's feet – a sign of respect normally given to the elderly. But, as she did with everyone, she pushed them gently away. Later in the day, more bands of poor villagers from both Uttar Pradesh and Madhya Pradesh came to greet Phoolan.

Watching Phoolan, I was struck by how cheerful she was. I had not been expecting this. The terrible things that had happened to her seemed not to have made her bitter. She could get angry and would occasionally scowl but in general she had a happy face. She often made what, although unintelligible to me, were obviously little jokes. She smiled a lot. She must have, I thought, tremendous inner strength.

Towards evening, a crowd of people began to gather in front of the house hoping to see Phoolan. There were several hundred of them. They were not at all threatening but the police soon moved them on.

I discussed Irène Frain's bestselling novel *Devi* with

Phoolan. She told me that Irène Frain had visited her in prison and asked about her life, but said nothing about being a writer. She had given Phoolan a watch when she left (this Phoolan subsequently gave away, not realising it was fairly valuable) and had not been in touch since. Phoolan gave me her address to see if I could get any money from her.

While we were having our evening meal, a herbal doctor brought medicine for Phoolan – I hoped it would not react with her other medication.

I rang Kamini Jaiswal to thank her for her help and to give her my itinerary. She was totally amazed that I was staying with Phoolan. She felt that Phoolan should relax with her family for a while. I could see that this was not very likely.

I said my farewells to Phoolan and to everyone else. Phoolan urged me to stay with them again when I returned to Delhi on the 25th. I left some of my things behind to collect then. Rameshchander gave me a lift to the station on his motorbike.

*

I left on the night train for Chennai (Madras). It was a journey of over thirteen hundred miles and lasted a day and a half. On the way, I casually asked some of my travelling companions for their opinion of Phoolan. They reckoned that she had killed at least a hundred and fifty people and thought that she should hang. I took care not to mention my connection with her.

While on the train, as we travelled through Karnataka, I went off to the toilet. The train then came to a halt and from outside there came the sound of stampeding feet and fighting. Through the toilet's frosted window I could see the silhouettes of people clambering along the outside of our coach. Then there was a tremendous din in the corridor. After a while I eased open the toilet door. As I did so, a pack of young shouting men fell backwards towards me into the cubicle. I thought

I might be crushed. Then the police arrived. There was much shouting and arguing. Suddenly, as quickly as they had arrived, the mob left. Shaken, I returned to my compartment. My fellow passengers looked traumatised. At one stage they had feared that, trapped as they were in a compartment where the windows could not be opened, they would suffocate. I learned that we had stopped at a station where a large crowd had been waiting for a train for a very long time. They had been bussed in for a political rally, promised return transport, and then abandoned. Seeing our relatively empty air-conditioned coach, they had stormed it. They had only left when another train had been found for them.

One of my companions told me that he had been in a similar incident in North India. There, when one of the passengers had remonstrated, he had been knifed to death.

'People are gentler in the south,' he remarked, with a grin. 'Here we only get asphyxiated!'

I travelled in Tamil Nadu for three weeks before returning to Delhi. As March progressed it became noticeably hotter. Midday temperatures were in the mid-thirties centigrade. When I had left Delhi the temperatures had been very pleasant, but on my return, although a little cooler than it had been in the south, it was much warmer. In my luggage there were numerous cotton saris to give the women in the house for the spring festival of Holi, and a water pistol.

*

I returned to Delhi on 25 March. As the train came into the capital, we halted at various signals. This gave an opportunity for beggars and pedlars to clamber aboard. I noticed some suspicious young men roaming the corridors. One, with a missing eye, looked like a film ruffian. He asked me in an unpleasantly aggressive way to give him money. He scowled when I refused.

A little later, as I stood in the corridor just outside my carriage, I felt the zip on my money belt being eased open from behind. I spun round to see the one-eyed man. I punched him in the face. He then ran away down the corridor with me in pursuit. The corridor was full of people waiting to disembark. As we sped through them, I shouted for someone to stop the would-be thief. No one helped. A Sikh army officer in my carriage, who had seen the whole episode, did not move. Later, when I berated him, he said calmly, 'It's normal in Delhi!' After a trip in the peaceful south, I knew I was back in the turbulent north.

Everywhere in Delhi there were stalls that displayed mounds of brightly coloured pigments on sale for the imminent festival of Holi. This celebration for the end of winter had similarities with All Fools' Day. The usual respect shown to elders and betters was briefly suspended to allow them to be daubed with pigment and dye. In some circles this was done in a restrained manner. However, many men drank copious quantities of bhang lassi, thin yoghurt laced with cannabis, and behaved outrageously. Women were liable to be groped and, in retaliation, men might be assaulted by women.

A bus from the railway station took me to Old Gupta Colony, where I arrived in the early afternoon. Near the house, under a sheet of corrugated iron, there was a shrine to Lord Hanuman, the monkey god. It was an almost formless block of stone, painted with red ochre and glistening with oil. It was popular with the users of a nearby open gym. TV crews were gathered around it. In their midst, I spotted the diminutive Phoolan. She waved at me to join her. She was in the middle of an interview for Jain TV. When she had finished, the interviewer asked me a few questions – who was I, where was I from, how did I know Phoolan? I tried to be as bland as possible – I did not have a police guard. Then Phoolan, myself, and all the women around, daubed each other's faces for Holi with red, yellow and blue pigment. As their cameras rolled, the men in the TV crews were daubed too. It was not exactly my idea of fun, but everyone else loved it.

Within the house, there were some changes. Rukhmani, Phoolan's elder sister had gone back to Gwalior. The youngest sister, Munni, had taken her place. She was about twenty, good-looking, and always smiling.

I was fed like a king as usual. The aubergine dish was very tasty. Like all the vegetables, they were lightly fried in oil to retain their flavour, not boiled in a sauce as I had been used to in the Bengali-style restaurants that abounded in London, and served with just-cooked piping-hot chapattis. It was amazing how the women managed to cook such excellent food, often for twenty or more, on a small two-ringed portable stove.

The sleeping arrangements had changed. It was necessary for me to share a large double bed with a younger cousin – not a thing I had done since I was a child. I knew, however, that the sharing of beds by those of the same sex was commonplace in India and would be something I would have to get used to. We were in an upstairs room with a huge fan blasting air over us. The fan kept the many mosquitoes away, but I really hated sleeping in a draught and never became used to it.

*

I woke up at 7 a.m. after a restless night – in the early hours, the fan had made the room too cold for me. There was no breakfast, but chapattis and vegetable dishes appeared about eleven. I went to the railway station to book my ticket for Jodhpur. I returned hoping for a quick doze, but that was impossible as the house was chock-full of visitors. We then set off for a cousin's village.

Phoolan was in a car with the driver, her immediate family and her bodyguard. The rest of us were in a Delhi municipality bus. Omprakesh drove it for a living and had 'borrowed' it for the day. The children had prepared buckets full of dye for Holi.

They were armed with large brass syringes. By chance, we left Delhi on the same road that the bus usually plied. There were groups of passengers waiting at the bus stops. As we approached them, the driver would slow down as if we were about to stop. The children, squealing with joy, would then completely soak all in the queue with the brilliant dyes before we accelerated away.

We stopped a few times along the way for Phoolan to be received by well-wishers. They garlanded her with marigolds and banknotes. Always there was a video camera in action. We then went to somebody's relative's restaurant for a snack. After that, we went to a neighbouring house for a reception and a full meal. Dozens of people crowded into the small room, where the old women put their hands on Phoolan's head to bless her. They also gave her bundles of money. I took some photographs.

Suddenly, one of the younger women came from behind and threw a large basin of blue dye all over me. Then the others followed suit. They drenched me with dye and smeared me with pigment. I was not too pleased since, at the women's insistence before we left Delhi, I had changed into my best clothes. These were ruined; I was wet through and cold. I tried to pretend I was enjoying things as much as everyone else. I fervently hoped that my camera had survived.

We then went to another house. A ceremony by a *sadhu* was in progress. We all sat on the floor in front of pictures of gods. The garlanded holy man periodically puffed a huge hookah and made soporific pronouncements.

When we left, I could not find the bus. Eventually, I ended up in someone's smoked-glass-windowed station wagon. I was taken back to the restaurant where we had been earlier and assured that our bus would turn up. It took ages. They found a bed for me to lie on – not that I could sleep with all the bustle. I suddenly realised that I had no idea where I was and started to wonder what I should do if I had been left behind. However, at

1 a.m. the bus eventually arrived and we got back to Delhi an hour or so later. Of course, everyone but me managed to sleep on the bus even though their heads were resting on the steel seat frames. It was extraordinary how Indians seemed to be able to sleep through any noise or discomfort and I envied them.

*

I was woken from my bed at 6 a.m. by the lights being switched on. Thereafter, there was much coming and going and it was impossible for me to get back to sleep. So I filled my water pistol with dye and used it to wake up those who were still asleep. Somewhat to my surprise, they loved it. I gave the women their saris. Everyone, especially Phoolan, was very pleased.

Then it was madness, with pigment and with dye. Everyone was attacked; everywhere was awash. Children and adults used pails, syringes and plastic-bag 'bombs'. I looked outside and saw that it was even wilder. The next-door yard was swimming in dye. Foolishly, I stepped outside. I was immediately attacked and had to take refuge in the police tent. By noon it was mostly over. I showered and changed, but some annoyingly late visitors then drenched me with dye again. I had no clean clothes left.

Still covered in pigment, Phoolan and I had our photo taken. Very surprisingly, for in many ways she adhered to traditional Indian behaviour, she asked me to put my arm around her. Once again, I was struck by how very small she was.

Some Muslim visitors came in the afternoon from a political party for the poor. Although Muslims do not observe Holi, they brought large boxes of congratulatory sweets.

In the evening, I took out my bottle of duty-free Johnnie Walker whisky. No one appeared to drink alcohol in the house except Harphool Singh, and he would only do it surreptitiously. He locked the two of us in his bedroom and we had a few tots. It was a good move on my part since, afterwards, with

Harphool Singh relaxed and affable, I was able to call for his son Rameshchander to come and translate a proper conversation.

Harphool Singh told me that he wanted Phoolan either to enter politics and become a member of the national parliament or of the Uttar Pradesh state legislative assembly, or else to set up national organisations for the lower castes and for women. He himself had stood at the last legislative assembly elections and wanted to become a MLA.* He told me that he was not too happy with Phoolan's behaviour, as he felt she was not always diplomatic and could be irresponsible. He said that she had recently gone off with her bodyguard and no one else, saying she would be back at 7 p.m. (There was still no sign of her when we went to bed.) I told him that in my opinion, to set anything up properly she would need the help of an able administrator. This would be essential since she was illiterate. He agreed, but seemed to have no idea of where anyone suitable might be found.

I promised Harphool Singh that I would speak to Phoolan about her future. Actually I had my doubts about Phoolan entering the political arena immediately. Such a move would raise her profile and was liable to enrage her enemies. They might try even harder to have her returned to jail. Moreover, she needed time to look around before deciding who she could trust. It would be best for her to proceed very slowly. I would try to talk things over with her, but as I needed an interpreter, I would have to tread carefully so as not to upset Harphool Singh. Ashokumar was away so I commandeered the bed in his room.

*

I woke at 7.45 a.m. feeling refreshed after the best night's sleep I had managed for a while. The adults were all up and about but

---

* India has a central federal parliament, whose members are called Member of Parliament (MP), and individual state assemblies, whose members are called Member of the Legislative Assembly (MLA).

the small children were still sleeping – the reverse of what happened back in Britain.

Phoolan finally returned mid-morning in the company of some officials from her caste, the Mallah. (She was not a Dalit, or 'Untouchable', as the media often reported, but from this boatmen community of the Sudra caste of labourers.) For a while, she was closeted with them and some other visitors. Then she came to see me, accompanied by a man from the caste organisation who spoke good English. We then had a most extraordinary conversation.

It seemed that Phoolan was not happy in the house – the women were bitchy to her and kept making snide remarks about marriage. Meanwhile, the Mallah men had advised her to marry, as she would find it difficult to mix socially if she were single. They had suggested that she get back with her old husband. I protested strongly when she told me this, but it turned out that they did not mean Putti Lal – the one who abused her so cruelly – but Man Singh, Phoolan's dacoit lover. Apparently Man Singh had been trying to contact her, but so far she had refused to see him. I pointed out to her that Man Singh had a bad reputation and that this might harm her rehabilitation. I also mentioned that he had no money.

Phoolan then took out a letter that offered marriage. It was from a man in Jammu Kashmir. He was a retired army officer, a widower with children. She said that she was thinking of accepting. The man from her caste offered to make enquiries. At one stage, Phoolan pulled out a postcard and instructed me to write to him and accept. I gently pointed out to her that Jammu Kashmir was very far away from her family. I also questioned what kind of person proposed by letter to someone with her background. I told her that I thought she should delay marriage for a while, since after she had settled down she would get better offers.

I wondered whether I had done the right thing. I found it

extraordinary that someone like me, with so little knowledge of India, was being asked for such advice. I had become used to advising Phoolan about her choice of lawyer and even about security and the risks of entering politics. Advice about marriage was another matter. Nevertheless, Phoolan seemed keen to know what I thought so I put aside my reservations.

I then suggested to Phoolan that she should move to Gwalior, live with her family, and go to the temple regularly to allay gossip. Amazingly, she agreed and said she would leave for Gwalior mid-April. She felt that security there would not be a problem. I wondered whether my relationship with Harphool Singh would now be difficult.

The man from Phoolan's caste told me that he would return on 8 April to discuss things further with Phoolan and me. I found it difficult to see her being married off willy-nilly. I was almost tempted to offer to enter into a marriage of convenience with her myself, but with the language and cultural problems it was not really a serious possibility. Also, even if she were allowed to immigrate, there would be too many difficulties facing an illiterate foreigner trying to live in the UK.

Maya and Sunita asked for my favourite dish and then cooked me okra for a late lunch. They also packed a few chapattis and vegetables for the train journey. Phoolan came downstairs to see me depart. I wondered whether I should be staying on to assist her. However, she folded her hands in a farewell namaste and I went. Omprakesh, the bus driver, had borrowed his bus again. He drove me in solitary splendour to Old Delhi railway station.

*

I travelled to Jodhpur and Jaisalmer in Rajasthan. I worried that Jain TV would transmit the pictures of Phoolan and me celebrating Holi, and that I would be recognised. They did broadcast the interview but, by an extraordinary and fortunate coincidence, an unseasonable thunderstorm in Jaisalmer caused a power failure there at transmission time. While there, I bought a silver necklace with a pendant of the goddess Durga for Phoolan.

*

A fortnight after my departure from Delhi, I returned to Old Gupta Colony. It was a nasty shock to find that the police had gone and that Phoolan was in hospital with what I was told was 'a heart problem'.

Phoolan had moved to a nearby relative's house the day after I had left. Apparently there had been a monumental row. She had accused Harphool Singh of using her for his own ambitions. Also, she had said that he was telling people that I had come to marry her. She had also accused the family of extracting saris and gifts from me. Taken aback, I made it plain I did not want to take sides. The main room looked bare with Phoolan's shrine gone.

The family tried to dissuade me from seeing Phoolan in hospital until after I had spoken to Rameshchander, who was due to return that night. I decided to go immediately. However, by mistake I ended up at the wrong hospital, the All India Institute of Medical Sciences, where they knew nothing of Phoolan. There were terrible traffic jams and pollution on the journey. I arrived back at the house tired and dispirited. Later, Rameshchander explained that the hospital I needed was the one on the opposite side of the road to the one that I had visited. I accepted his offer to drive me there first thing the next morning. I slept downstairs, exhausted.

*

At 8 a.m. I went with Rameshchander to the correct hospital. We were directed to an 'Intensive Cardiac Care Unit – no visitors admitted'. Eventually, after an hour or so, I prevailed upon the doctor to let me in for a few minutes. Phoolan, looking grey, was delighted to see me. She was quiet at first, as instructed by the doctor. Soon, however, she was leaping up with excitement to show me a letter from a French publisher.

The letter offered to pay her expenses to go to Paris to discuss a ghosted autobiography. A draft contract was enclosed. In essence, this offered Phoolan one-third of the co-author royalties, with the right of editorial control. It looked good to me and, watched by the bemused nurses, I told her so. I promised her that I would telephone the publishers.

Phoolan was in the middle of making some remarks about how evil Harphool Singh was, when I was thrown out. The doctor said that he had only allowed me in as a special concession. He insisted that Phoolan must rest and that I must go. Before I went, I gave Phoolan a shawl and the silver Devi necklace. Her face lit up. As I walked away, not knowing if she would recover, I felt overwhelmingly sad.

I spoke to the police guard outside the ward, who surprisingly was armed only with a pistol, and obtained Phoolan's new address. I took a taxi. At the house, there was a tent outside and I received a big welcome from my police friends. They playfully aimed their rifles at me. They told me that Munni and Santosh had gone off to the hospital. I left a message to say that I would return at 4 p.m., and then went to Old Gupta Colony, only a couple of miles away, and packed. It was awkward parrying Maya Devi's questions. I then returned to Phoolan's house.

There was no one there at first and I rested for a while on one of the police beds. Then her cousin who owned the house arrived. Nashu Ram Nishad was blind, but had a good teaching job. He spoke fair English and we chatted. Suddenly, out of the blue, the tone of his voice changed.

'What are your intentions towards my cousin?' he asked.

He used the stiff English phrase as he might have read it in a Victorian novel. I was stunned, but soon recovered enough to give a calm reply.

'My intentions? Why, merely to help her. To me, she is like a sister.'

There was a slightly awkward pause. Then fortunately we were disturbed by the arrival of some guests. It was his child's naming day – twelve days after the birth – and friends had come with celebratory sweets.

*

I telephoned Kamini Jaiswal to discuss the proposal for Phoolan's book. She said that Phoolan would not get a passport to travel while her court case was pending. She had also told me that the outcome of the cases in Uttar Pradesh was still uncertain. The Chief Minister might eventually pardon her, but his own position was precarious. In the end, matters would have to be decided in the Supreme Court. Kamini seemed uncertain as to whether in the meantime Phoolan would have to go back to prison. She thought that everything would be finalised over the next couple of months. With regard to the book, we agreed that I should speak to the French publisher first. Afterwards, she would discuss matters with Phoolan and deal with the legal side of any contract.

I had just finished speaking when, to my utter amazement, Munni and Santosh arrived – followed by Phoolan. I was stunned. How could Phoolan be out of intensive care? By some miracle, she seemed to be fully recovered and her usual energetic self.

I had a long talk with Phoolan. We discussed the book proposal. We agreed that I should suggest to the publisher that they send a co-author to India, and that later Phoolan would go to France for the launch. I asked her about her plans. She told me that Shiv Narayan, her brother, was coming the next week to discuss matters. She might, perhaps, move to Gwalior. Meanwhile, she would raise some money for social work. I asked if this would give her an income for herself. She said that it would. In any case, she added, she could always rely on people to give her enough money for her needs. Having seen the way so many people idolised her, I realised that this was true.

I then asked Phoolan about the row with Harphool Singh.

'He was using me for his own political ambitions,' Phoolan said. 'He tried to control who I should meet. He even woke me up in the middle of the night and asked me to phone Mulayam Singh to suggest that he be made the president of the local party.'

'And is it true that there was talk of me having come to marry you?'

'Yes. The women talked about it constantly. I told them that you had no such idea. You had made that clear. But they went on about it. That was why I stayed away on the night of Holi. I did not want to appear too familiar with you.'

I wondered whether Phoolan had exaggerated the difficulties with Harphool Singh's family. She was probably a little too sensitive after being in jail so long. They had certainly been extremely good to me and I hoped that it would be possible for me to remain friendly with them.

'I'm sorry if it caused you any embarrassment,' I said.

'They were to blame. Now, I want to ask you a question.'

'Yes?'

'I've been told that in London the old are not properly respected. Is that true?'

'Well, not so respected as in India.'

'In that case, when you retire you must come to live here. I will see that you are well looked after.' She gave me a big smile. 'You can rely on me.'

We said our final goodbyes. A taxi was summoned. I gave Phoolan one last piece of advice before I set off to collect my luggage from Old Gupta Colony and go on to the airport.

'Be extremely careful about your security!'

4
Bandit Queen

*'How does Shekhar Kapur have the right
to show me being raped?'*

A WEEK after my return to London in April 1994, I rang
Susanna Lea, the foreign-rights manager of the publisher
Robert Laffont, in Paris. Just a few days earlier, she had
happened to be in Delhi and had already met with Phoolan. All
seemed to be progressing satisfactorily. She did not say cate-
gorically that the book was going ahead, but it sounded very
hopeful, and she had agreed with my suggestion that it would
be more sensible to write the book in India. She seemed
very sympathetic towards Phoolan. She had also met Kamini
Jaiswal, which was good. She added that she would look into
the Irène Frain business to see if anything could be done about
getting something for Phoolan.

I wrote to Phoolan. I mentioned that I had started to take
Hindi lessons, so that we could speak without an interpreter.
(This was a bit hopeful given my aptitude for languages.) I told
her that I had contacted the French publisher and continued:

I think you should try to do this project if the price is right.
This book could give you enough to live simply on. You will not
have to ask other people for money, and will be independent.
This is very important for you.

I was very glad that you have decided to do samaj seva
[social work]. When you have done this for some time you will

understand politics better. At the moment politics is too
dangerous for you. Do samaj seva and keep your ears and eyes
open. That way you will learn which politicians can be trusted.

It was marvellous that we met this time. I was hoping that
you would be released before I came, but, of course, I could
not be sure. Your case may take a long time to conclude, but
meanwhile you are free. Do not say anything to make people
angry. Above all, do what Kamini Jaiswal tells you.

I also wrote a thank you letter to Rameshchander and sent a
little present to Kamini Jaiswal – *The Oxford Book of Legal
Anecdotes*.

*

A few weeks later, I received a letter from Phoolan. Her health
was quite good and she had signed a contract with the French
publisher. She had moved into a flat in Gulmohar Park – a
smart area of south Delhi – which they were paying for. So, I
thought, that had all turned out very well.

*

On Friday 13 May, a friend telephoned me to say that there had
been an article in the previous day's *Evening Standard* on the
film about Phoolan. I rushed out to the newsagent's but the
unsold copies had already been returned. However, a customer
in the shop said that she had a copy and she dropped it in later.
There was a full-page enthusiastic review of *Bandit Queen*.
It described the film, directed by Shekhar Kapur, as 'a truly
radical film' which was set to capture the Cannes Film Festival
the following week and that it would show that 'Indian cinema
has at last grown up'.

Whatever its merits, I was uneasy at the descriptions
of sexual violence – 'raped by her husband in a shocking

sequence; stripped stark naked and paraded publicly through the village'. Was it, I wondered, too graphic for Phoolan to see? How would people who had seen it treat her? I was not at all sure that I could bear to see it myself. Maybe, as the article suggested was probable, the censors would demand cuts. There were similarly enthusiastic reviews in other newspapers.

Ten days later, a friend in Los Angeles sent me an article in the *Hollywood Reporter* written by their correspondent at the Cannes Film Festival. Headed '"Bandit Queen" Steals Scene', it predicted that the film was 'about to cause massive problems for censors all over the world as the producers, Film Four International, report feverish interest from distributors . . . Whatever the film's reception in Cannes, its brutal realism is certain to cause huge problems in both the subcontinent and in Western territories such as Great Britain, the latter in the grip of censorship fever over screen violence . . . the central rape scene will cause ratings problems because Phoolan Devi was no more than a child of 11 at the time of the forced marriage.'

The *Hollywood Reporter* article confirmed my worst fears about the film. I was sure that Phoolan would be terribly distressed. What rape victim wants to have her agony re-enacted on cinema screens across the world? I wrote to Phoolan:

> The film 'Bandit Queen' was shown at the film festival in France. It is expected to open here in September. Several of the film critics in the English newspapers say it is very good. They say it shows you in a good light. However, they also say the film is very violent. There are many scenes of you being abused and raped.
>
> Phoolan, you must think very hard before you decide to see this film. It will be very upsetting for you. I am not saying you should see it, or not see it. That is your decision. But, think very hard. Even I may decide not to see it. It will be upsetting for me too.

*

I saw nothing more about the film for several months. I had also heard nothing from Phoolan. Unfortunately, I had no phone number for her new residence. On 22 July there was a small piece about Phoolan in the *Independent* – saying that she 'has slipped out of the public eye and into a life of domesticity . . . Ms Devi disclosed her recent marriage to her sister's ex-husband.' I could not work out exactly who this might be, unless perhaps the widower of her dead sister. A few weeks later, I found an article in an Indian weekly that was available in London, *India Today*. It reported that she had married an Umed Singh. There was a photograph, from which I recognised the face of a visitor to Harphool Singh's house. Phoolan was quoted as saying that her marriage was 'a community decision'. I thought maybe it was a good idea, and certainly better than her marrying one of the more unsuitable men who had been suggested. I only hoped that he would be good to her.

Next day, I dropped into the Indian restaurant to see Ajit. He showed me an article in an Indian newspaper, written in Punjabi, which reported that Phoolan was going to the Indian courts to try to stop the showing of *Bandit Queen*.

On 30 August the *Independent* carried an article on Phoolan's fight against the film. It reported that she had threatened to set herself on fire if *Bandit Queen* was released in India without her being allowed to see it and then giving her permission. 'They have shown me naked to the press. People come up to me and say I look very sexy. I find all this humiliating. Kapur and Bedi want to cheat me. They want to use my name to sell a fake story to the world. Why else haven't they shown it to me?' Sandeep Singh Bedi, the producer, was quoted as saying that he was prepared to show it to her in private.

I was shocked by Phoolan's threat to kill herself. Given her past, it struck me that it was something she really might do. I was also amazed to learn that the film had been shown at Cannes and in Delhi without Phoolan even being allowed to see it first. I wrote to her. After congratulating her on her marriage, I continued:

> I also hear that you are trying to stop 'Bandit Queen' being shown in India without your permission. I hope you are successful in this. However, sister Phoolan, if you cannot stop it, do not upset yourself too much. Because of untrue stories they have heard about your past, some people in India are always going to be against you. But, you know yourself that you have done nothing wrong. Also there are very many people in India, and abroad, who respect you. So be happy about that, and do not be too depressed.

On 9 September, the BBC reported that Phoolan had won the first round in her court case to stop the film being shown in India. The Delhi High Court had imposed a temporary ban.

A Canadian friend sent me a cutting from the *Toronto Star* of 11 September. The film was to be screened that day at the Toronto International Film Festival. It reported that Phoolan had sent a letter to the organisers asking them not to show it. They were, however, going ahead. The festival director said he was satisfied that the film was based on Phoolan's own testimony. Shekhar Kapur, the film's director, said he was certain Phoolan had not seen the film and insisted that all the events depicted were true – 'and with everyone jumping on her bandwagon now, I don't know how much control she has on her own life. I think she is being manipulated.' Meanwhile, in India the authorities were demanding the cut of thirty scenes before they would allow the film to be released.

On 8 October I received a letter from Phoolan. It was dated 24 September, from B-99 Gulmohar Park, New Delhi, and written by someone in poor and almost indecipherable English. The bits I could read said something like:

I received your letter and am very glad you and your family are quite well. My health is very poor and I'm in pain.

Yes it is true I am married with Umed Singh. My husband is very smart and beautiful gentleman. You come just now for meet my husband.

I am not giving the permission 'Bandit Queen' picture for show.

There was a postscript, mostly in Hindi, which Ajit read out to me:

Respected Brother, Roy Moxham, the film 'Bandit Queen' about Phoolan Devi has been made. It is not truthful. Please try and oppose the film with this letter, which is in the handwriting of my husband Umed Singh. I wait to hear from you.

Many thanks,

Phoolan Devi

Umed Singh

I mulled things over for a couple of days. I discussed options with friends. It would be complicated to write to all the various licensing authorities in the UK and impossible to do so to those overseas. I decided that the best course of action would be to write to the chief executive of Channel 4, Michael Grade. I did this on 11 October and enclosed a copy of Phoolan's authorisation to act for her:

I write on behalf of my friend, Phoolan Devi, to beg you to self-censor the C4 film of her life, 'Bandit Queen' . . . .

She is very distressed to think that she will be shown elsewhere in the world in the nude, and in explicit sexual scenes. She has already been taunted by people . . .

She is worried:

1. That the film will be seen in world cinemas, and that she will be humiliated. Also many people may see the film

outside India, and then go back there. She herself may travel abroad and be despised.

2. It will be shown on world TV, with similar results. However, it may then also be video-recorded, and find its way back to India.

3. It will be sold as a video, with similar consequence . . . .

If your company were to make a film about a live Englishwoman, who had been abused and raped, you would never have been so insensitive. Cannot you show similar compassion for a woman from India? She has suffered enough already. Could you please have the more offensive scenes cut, to avoid giving her more pain?

I found myself waiting impatiently for a reply. When I telephoned C4, a supercilious secretary told me – 'We get lots of letters. You'll get a reply in due course.'

Before I did get a reply, I was sent two articles that had appeared in the Calcutta magazine *Sunday*. Arundhati Roy, a scriptwriter (who would go on to win the Booker Prize for *The God of Small Things*) had written them. They were headed 'The Great Indian Rape-Trick', and were extremely scathing about the film and its creators. The pieces accused them of radically departing from the truth, or from even the version in Mala Sen's book:

Every time the Director has been faced with something that could disrupt the simple, pre-fabricated calculations of his cloying morality play, it has been tampered with and *forced* to fit.

Arundhati Roy wrote that in front of herself Phoolan had telephoned the producer to ask when she could see the film and could not obtain a definite date.

On the one hand the concerned cowboys Messers Bedi and Kapur are so eager to share with us the abject humiliation and domination of Phoolan Devi's 'soul,' and on the other hand they seem to be totally uninterested in her. In what she thinks of the film, or what the film will do to her life and future. What is she to them? A *concept*? Or just a cunt?*

Another article was in the bestselling *India Today*. Captioned 'The Truth on Trial', it pointed out that the film opened with the claim that it was 'the true story of Phoolan Devi'. However, it reported, the film deviated considerably from Mala Sen's book, although it had been scripted by her, in order to put more emphasis on animosity between the high castes and the low castes. It failed to mention that Phoolan's initial troubles had actually come from relatives in her own low caste. It had invented an upper-caste molester of Phoolan in the village, who had never actually existed. In an interview, Phoolan confirmed this. She added, 'What I object to is that when I can't even talk to another woman about rape, how does Shekhar Kapur have the right to show me being raped?'

Even more seriously, the film depicted Phoolan as being present at the Behmai massacre. She was shown shooting villagers in the legs. She was shown as commanding her gang when men were lined up and killed. Phoolan had strongly denied being directly involved. She had vehemently insisted that she was elsewhere, both to the police at her surrender and in Mala Sen's book. I feared that these scenes in the film would not only prejudice a trail, but would provoke retribution. Taken together with the manipulated message of the film – that Phoolan was advocating violence towards the upper castes – some members of those castes would feel obliged to act. They might kill her.

* Full text on: http://www.sawnet.org/books/writing/roy_bq1.html

I again telephoned C4 and was again told that I would get a reply in due course. Toward the end of October, it was announced that *Bandit Queen* would be shown in the London Film Festival in early November.

On 1 November, I finally received a reply from Michael Grade. It sought to counter my points about the effect of the film on Phoolan by referring to her working on her autobiography – a book, of course, not yet written and whose content was unknown. The letter concentrated on Channel 4's legal rights. It asserted that the film had been made with Phoolan's 'complete cooperation' and that she had received money. Channel 4 would, he wrote, oppose Phoolan's efforts to censor the film with 'the utmost vigour'. There was not one word of sympathy for Phoolan.

I found this rejection most depressing. I had, I supposed, been naive in imagining that an appeal to compassion would help Phoolan. I should have realised that it would be fruitless once the moneymen and the lawyers had become involved. I was angry too. To give vent to my feeling I wrote back a stinging reply: 'She may have cooperated in the making of *a* film, but certainly not *this* film. Are you seriously saying that she agreed to a film depicting her in nude and rape scenes? . . . Much as you plead justification, you know full well that these scenes will compound the harm done to this woman.'

After I calmed down, I scanned the C4 letterhead's list of directors to see if there might be someone more sympathetic. An Indian name stood out: Usha Prashar (later to become chairman of the Parole Board of England and Wales and a life peer). I wrote to her. Eventually I received back a one-line reply that she had nothing to add to Michael Grade's letter.

The first showing of *Bandit Queen*, as part of the London Film Festival, was on 4 November in Leicester Square. It was in the afternoon, so that as I was working in Canterbury, it would have been difficult for me to attend. In any case, I did not think

I could face seeing it. My friend Sharada agreed to go and give me a report, and we spoke that evening. She said that the film was very well made and broadly sympathetic to Phoolan. However, it depicted all her problems as having been instigated by the upper castes. More importantly, there were many, many graphic rape scenes, replete with Phoolan's screams. Both Shekhar Kapur and Mala Sen spoke at the showing. They confirmed that the film was blocked by the censors in India but failed to mention Phoolan's own objections.

By showing the film in the festival, C4 had avoided having to obtain a certificate from the British Board of Film Classification – which they would need in order to put the film on general release. I wrote to the Board, enclosing copies of Phoolan's authority to me and of the correspondence with Michael Grade – 'This is a film about a living person. If she were an English rape victim it would never have been made. I ask you to insist on the cutting of the material that will further aggravate the injury done to Phoolan Devi, or refuse a certificate.'

I also wrote to the Broadcasting Standards Council and the Independent Television Commission to try and stop any attempt to put the film out on television. I pointed out that this would be video-recorded and sent back to India. I realised that these initiatives, even if fruitful, would not achieve what I had asked of C4. There were many other countries where the film might be released and I could not tackle all of them.

I wrote to Phoolan to tell her what I had done. I tried to soften the blow of Channel 4's intransigence – 'The film, although it shows things it should not, and is not properly truthful, does make people sympathetic to you. Many of these well-educated people thought you were just a murderer. Now they see that it was you who was wronged.'

The Broadcasting Standards Council and the Independent Television Commission both replied to me to say that they were unable to do anything prior to any transmission. They might take action after the film had gone out, but that would be of little comfort to me or to Phoolan. Repeated phone calls to the British Board of Film Classification, where a secretary confirmed they had received my letter, failed to produce any response. It seemed to me that all these so-called regulators were just so much window dressing, providing jobs for 'the great and the good'.

Early in December there was an article in the *Guardian* by Mala Sen. She had made an emotional reunion with Phoolan shortly after her release. However, after the film was shown, things had changed. She wrote that Phoolan had told her, 'You have shown filthy things about me.' Mala had then replied, 'But gang rape *is* filthy, Phoolan.' In the court case to ban the film, Kamini Jaiswal was acting for Mala. 'I feel very saddened by the whole affair,' Mala wrote. So did I, for Mala had been of great help to Phoolan. The greatest pity was, I thought, that Mala had been swayed into straying, for cinematic effect, from the account in her own book.

At the beginning of 1995, I began to pick up signals that there were problems in obtaining finance to extend my contract at Canterbury Cathedral Archives. It would expire at the end of August. Kent County Council, which together with the Cathedral funded my post, was planning severe cuts. I began to consider my options. One was that I might go to do conservation work in India for a while. When self-employed, I had done a lot of work on Islamic books, and many Mughal and other treasures in India were in dire need of conservation. I wrote to a number of Indian cultural institutions and to the British Council in Delhi to see if there were any possibilities.

One day in the middle of January I booked a flight to Delhi, to travel out on 18 February and return on 2 April. That day, I visited the British Board of Film Classification in Soho Square. The secretary to James Firman, the director, told me that *Bandit*

Queen had already been classified 18. I was stunned. She could offer no clue as to why my letter and repeated phone calls had been ignored. That very same day, I went to see *Amateur* at the Renoir Cinema. I walked into the cinema into the middle of a trailer for *Bandit Queen*. It was as offensive as I had imagined. All my efforts had come to naught.

Once my ticket was booked I made valiant efforts to learn more Hindi. This was still very basic. I ruefully recalled getting seventeen per cent in GCE 'O'-level French. Much of the vocabulary I strove to master was not in the usual beginner's list – 'rape', 'censor', 'injunction', 'judgment'.

At the beginning of February I was told that because of the council's financial position my contract at the archive would definitely not be renewed. This coincided with a letter from the Indian National Trust for Art and Heritage inviting me to get in touch with them when I came to Delhi. The British Council also suggested that I visit.

In the week that I left Britain, *Bandit Queen* opened in cinemas nationwide.[*] Two days before I left, there was a piece in the *Guardian* by Derek Malcolm in which Shekhar Kapur, the *Bandit Queen* director, sought to justify his position: 'I've tried to shoot Phoolan's unstructured, relentless world as she might have viewed it, sometimes based on her own words and sometimes on my interpretation of what she was hiding behind the words of her dictated prison diaries. All I can say is that, as a man, I've done my best to understand.' He now admits it might

---

[*] I never managed to steel myself to watch 'Bandit Queen' during all the years I knew Phoolan. I had no wish to see the rape of a friend. In 2009 I felt that, as now I was writing of what had happened, I should see it. I did not want any of those involved to profit from my action, so I viewed a DVD that I imagined was pirated. It was a most unpleasant experience. It confirmed all that I had been told and supposed about the film's treatment of the facts. These had indeed been altered so as to fit the film's message of caste conflict. The opening caption 'This is a True Story' was a complete travesty.

have been wiser to make the film without appending any names or claiming any basis of truth.

*

I flew out of London on the morning of 18 February, but a mechanical fault and a subsequent stopover en route meant that I did not reach Delhi until 5 a.m. on 20 February. I dozed on an airport seat for a while, washed and shaved, and took a taxi to south Delhi. Gulmohar Park was a typically pleasant middle-class area of Delhi. Its clean streets were lined with flowering trees. Behind small front gardens there were small detached blocks of apartments. Phoolan's block had four flats, painted white, with balconies. From a balcony on the first floor a man looked down into the street. He was dressed in unremarkable Western-style trousers and shirt. Something about his appearance, though, perhaps his posture or his haircut, immediately suggested to me that he was a policeman. I called up to him, in English. He affected not to have heard me. I tried Hindi and, after a while, obtained his attention. I told him that I was a friend of Phoolan's. He obviously did not believe me, probably thinking that I was a journalist. Eventually he waved me up. I had to wait a while, and then he went inside to talk to someone. At 9 a.m. I was led into the flat. It was very bare inside, with just a sprinkling of old furniture. I was ushered into the far room. Umed and Phoolan lay in bed.

Phoolan was delighted to see me. Umed, too, made me very welcome. He was a thickset man in his thirties, with a moustache, a nice smile and an easy manner. He had some English. I gathered that he was not, as had been reported, the ex-husband of one of Phoolan's sisters, but merely an acquaintance of Harphool Singh. Phoolan's younger sister, Munni, was also there and glad to see me again. Her baby boy, Lalu, crawled on the floor. Later, her quiet husband Hargobind would return from work.

Meanwhile, it was obvious that I was tired and I was sent off to one of the three bedrooms to doze for much of the morning.

After lunch we caught up on each other's news. I gathered that Phoolan's autobiography was nearly ready for release in France, and that a German edition was also on its way. It seemed that Umed had a block of land near the airport that he was sub-dividing and building upon. Property prices in India, and especially in Delhi, had risen dramatically over recent years. I feared that the bubble might burst soon and hoped it would not take Umed and Phoolan's savings with it. Early in the evening, I was shown a video of political rally in Bihar, where Phoolan was the main speaker. There were literally hundreds of thousands of people there to hear her. It was extraordinary to think that only the year before she had been in jail.

Phoolan's appearance had changed. She was no longer the frail waif-like figure of the previous year. Her face and figure had filled out. Everywhere she went people offered her snacks. Sweets were continually pushed on her. Not that she needed much urging. After so long in jail, she was happy to indulge herself. Moreover, she took very little exercise. She still had various stomach pains, which would have made that difficult. In any case, for security reasons she normally had to be driven around.

When she came out of jail she was much thinner than when she went in. At the surrender she was extremely fit, having spent years evading the police in the Chambal ravines. She had often walked twenty-five miles or more a day, while carrying a heavy gun and ammunition. She told me that the reason that she became so thin in prison was because she had contracted tuberculosis, and had for a long time been refused medical treatment. Now, she looked about her right weight, but I feared that further indulgence and lack of exercise might take its toll.

When I first met Phoolan she had just come out of jail and was living in the houses of others. Her speech then had been restrained, even demure. Now that she had been lauded everywhere and was mistress of her own house, her manner was more assertive, her tone more commanding. For the first time I saw her lose her temper. Some political associate would make a mistake and she would lambaste him. I knew that Phoolan was famous for her use of inventive swearing. During her time as a dacoit there had been many reports of her taunting the police by threatening to mutilate their private parts. Most of her Hindi abuse was beyond me, and no one was keen to translate it. Nevertheless, I often heard her use the two Hindi words I did know – 'sister-fucker' and 'cunt'. (The first I knew because it was used so commonly; the second because I had once uttered it by mistake, instead of the similar-sounding word for holiday.) She knew, however, when this might be acceptable and when not. If necessary she could speak very properly.

*

Later that evening Phoolan, Umed and I, together with one or two bodyguards, went for dinner to the flat of the government Minister for Minorities. He was dressed in the saffron robes of a Buddhist.

There were a couple of other men there and also a Buddhist abbot from Darjeeling. I was totally amazed to learn from him that earlier in the month Phoolan had decided to convert to Buddhism. It astonished me because I had always seen Phoolan as being quintessentially Hindu. On my last visit to India she had been almost obsessive in her devotion to the shrine she had built for numerous images of the Hindu goddess Durga. But then I remembered that when in prison she had written to tell me that she was thinking of changing her religion and had asked me for my advice. I knew that Buddhism, recently almost extinct in India, the land of its birth, had been given a major impetus by the conversion of many Dalits, 'Untouchables'. Phoolan was not, of course, a Dalit, but like them she was strongly opposed to the Hindu caste system. So, I reasoned, perhaps her conversion was not that surprising. Moreover, there was no animosity from the Hindus towards Buddhists, for, when Buddhism had been absorbed back into Hinduism, the Buddha had become one of the gods of the Hindus.

The meal was of fish soup, a large boiled fish, fried chicken, rice and vegetables. Phoolan helped herself to rice and vegetables. Then the minister scooped the fish head out of the soup and dumped it on top of her pile of vegetables. I was startled because I knew that Phoolan was strictly vegetarian. Then, to my astonishment, she calmly ate it. Later she had some chicken too.

'I thought that Buddhists were vegetarian,' I said to the abbot.

'Not at all,' he replied. 'We should eat any food that we are given.'

After the meal Phoolan was presented with a book on Buddhism and, more usefully, with a statue of Lord Buddha. She was also given a large bundle of banknotes, presumably for her social causes. The abbot invited me to stay in his Darjeeling monastery. We left at 10 p.m. Surrounded by the religious conversation at dinner, most of it in Hindi that I did not understand, I had nearly nodded off, so I was glad to get to bed relatively early.

I slept soundly. Everyone seemed to rise very late for an Indian household. It was 9 a.m. before I heard Munni moving about, and 10 a.m. by the time Phoolan and Umed appeared. Shortly afterwards, the Buddhist minister arrived and began earnest discussions with Phoolan. He told me than Phoolan and he were trying to construct a 'minorities' coalition of the religious minorities and the lower castes. This would, if realised, make up a majority of the population. Meanwhile, he had a plan to build a training institute for activists, close to Delhi but in Uttar Pradesh. He envisioned a really big organisation, with Phoolan as its director.

Phoolan Devi formally surrenders at Bhind, 12 February 1983
(© *Sondeep Shankar/AP/Press Association Images*).

The author by the entrance to Phoolan Devi's family home. Ghura ka Purva, 1996.

Ramkali, Phoolan's younger sister, milking the water-buffalo. Ghura ka Purva, 199

above left: Phoolan Devi's first letter to the author, dated 29 June 1992.

above right: Photograph of Phoolan copied on to her letter to the author from Gwalior jail, dated 16 October 1992. Her signature is underneath.

right: Phoolan Devi with the author covered in pigment, at Holi. Delhi, 1994.

Shiv Narayan, Phoolan Devi's brother, with his wife, Shoba. Gwalior, 1993.

Munni, Phoolan's youngest sister, at the family shrine. Gulmohar Park, Delhi, 1995.

Phoolan Devi accepting book and a statue of the Buddha from the Minister for Minorities. Her husband, Umed Singh (centre). Delhi, 1995.

Phoolan cleaning the flat. Gulmohar Park, Delhi, 1995.

Above: Moola, Phoolan Devi's mother, with Jacki Delhi, 1996.

Left: Rukhmani, Phoolan's elder sister. Gwalior, 1999.

Phoolan Devi puts a *tilak* on the author's forehead, with her brother Shiv Narayan looking on. Gwalior, 1999.

A view of Chitrakut, 1999.

Left: Phoolan Devi campaigning for women, 1995 (© *Kapoor Baldev/ Sygma/Corbis*).

Below: Sonia Gandhi, Congress President, paying her respects to Phoolan's body, 2001 (© *Kapoor Baldev/Sygma/ Corbis*).

'She could,' he told me, his eyes bright with enthusiasm, 'become another Mother Teresa!'

I had my doubts about that. Nevertheless, I thought, even if the institute turned out to be less grandiose than he planned it might prove to be a good springboard for Phoolan.

Later in the day a journalist came to interview Phoolan. After the interview he stunned me by saying that Phoolan had now decided not to convert to Buddhism. Apparently, a large hall had already been hired for the ceremony. Also a considerable number of dignitaries had accepted invitations. The Minister of Minorities would, I imagined, not be pleased.

Later, I asked Phoolan why she had changed her mind.

'I asked if it was true, what I had heard,' she said, 'that a Buddhist should forgive her enemies. When they told me, "Yes, it is," I decided not to convert!'

When not busy with meetings and interviews, Phoolan liked to help with the housework. She would prepare vegetables, help with the cooking and sweep the floors. She particularly enjoyed looking after and bathing Munni's son and the various other children who turned up.

I went to the railway station and bought tickets for my departure on the 24th to Calcutta (now Kolkata) and various places on the way. It was raining heavily and unexpectedly cold for late February. When I returned to Gulmohar Park, Shiv Narayan, Phoolan's brother, had arrived together with two friends from Gwalior. He had been cool toward me when we last met in 1992, but this time he was far more cordial. I went to bed early and left the other three, who would eventually sleep on my floor, playing cards.

*

Next morning I had an appointment with an official of the British Council to discuss the possibilities of them providing funding for a conservation post in India for me. The prospects were better than before and it seemed that it might be possible. I then went to the offices of the Indian National Trust for Art and Cultural Heritage (INTACH), where I met the secretary, Martand Singh. He was most helpful. He arranged for me to meet with their head of conservation in Lucknow the following week. INTACH's offices were in the splendid grounds of the huge mausoleum of Humayun, the sixteenth-century Mughal emperor. It was one of my favourite buildings and I took the opportunity to view it again. Between INTACH and the tomb was normally a Boy Scouts' camp. Rather bizarrely, it had now been taken over by the 'Children of God', the cult implicated in Europe and America in the 'flirty fishing' scandal, when sex had been used as bait for recruiting converts.

When I returned to the flat it was crammed with people. Mats had been spread over the living-room floor. Framed and garlanded pictures of Dr Ambedkar, the Dalit leader who had written the Indian constitution that had outlawed 'untoucha-bility', were propped against the walls. On the mats and chairs sat about thirty representatives of the Dalits and 'backward classes' – a term used to describe various designated castes, tribes and 'other backward classes' who were entitled to some positive discrimination. There were delegates from Uttar Pradesh, Bihar, Rajasthan and the Punjab. There were Hindus, Muslims, Buddhists, Christians and Animists. There were some women but the vast majority were men. It was extraordinary to see how such a tiny woman as Phoolan could dominate such a meeting with her charisma. Several documents were read out to Phoolan. If she approved of the contents, she then laboriously appended her signature. I was asked to take photo-graphs. This took a while as people wanted to smarten up first. One man insisted on changing into a white shirt and trousers that were so stiffly starched that they could only be opened with great difficulty. When I had finished, I took everyone's home address so that I could send each a print.

It was a quiet evening. Phoolan looked tired. The young men played cards and watched Bollywood films. I went to bed and tried to sleep.

*

Next morning, a reporter for the German magazine *Stern* came to conduct an interview. He was accompanied by an Indian photographer living nearby who acted as translator. This photographer had been present at Phoolan's surrender in 1983. Initially the reporter was hostile to Phoolan, but as the interview went on he gradually warmed to her. She talked of her time in jail and of how she now intended to campaign for better prison conditions. She described how girls had been set up to be imprisoned and then bailed out by rich men for sex; of how girls were forcibly taken away to the prison officers' houses for sex. She described how, although the 'bandits' were kept in a separate part of the jail, a condition Phoolan had demanded before her surrender, other women inmates would come into her section to help with the cleaning and then tell her what was going on. Once, when a girl was telling Phoolan of some horror, a male jailer stripped the girl in front of Phoolan and beat her. Phoolan said that she then punched the prison officer in the face and broke some of his teeth. The *Stern* reporter looked sceptical until Baldev, the translator, told him that at Phoolan's surrender, when he himself had got too close, she had attacked him and smashed his camera.

Phoolan then outlined her plans to establish an organisation for the backward classes. It was to be called Eklavya Sena – the army of Eklavya, a character in the Mahabharata. In that ancient epic, Eklavya was an archer of lowly origin. He requested tuition from Drona, the tutor of Prince Arjuna. Because of his low birth, this was refused. By self-study, Eklavya taught himself to be an outstanding archer; so outstanding that he might have surpassed the ability of Drona's favourite student, Arjuna. Drona then sought out Eklavya. When Eklavya prostrated himself before Drona, he was asked for the gift that a student must give to the teacher before completing their training. Eklavya humbly agreed. Drona then asked Eklavya for his thumb. Though aware that it would ruin his ability as an archer, Eklavya meekly cut off his own thumb.

Some Hindus saw the story as a parable to illustrate the respect due to a teacher. The backward classes, however, saw it as an example of how, by cunning, the upper ranks of society had managed to dominate them.

Phoolan said that each member of the new 'army' would have a symbolic bow and arrow. It would be a consciousness-raising organisation rather than a political party.

'How many do you intend to enrol?' the reporter asked her.

'I don't know.'

'You must have some idea – a thousand, ten thousand . . . '

'Perhaps a few crore.'

'What's a crore?'

He looked astounded when it was explained to him that a crore was ten million.

In the afternoon we went off to see the Mughal Gardens, the spectacular ornamental garden of the President of India. This was only opened to the public in February and March. As invariably happened, we left behind schedule. We were then further delayed by running into the chaos that regularly occurred in Delhi as roads were sealed off to allow the Prime Minister's convoy to pass unimpeded by traffic. We arrived just as the garden's gates were being closed, too late to gain admittance. We then went to a market for vegetables, where our accompanying bodyguard made himself inconspicuous and Phoolan was not recognised. She proved to be a formidable bargainer.

We spent a quiet evening at home. 'Quiet' was probably the

wrong word since the telephone, which had been disconnected in some dispute over the bill, had been reconnected. The press were delighted and it was in constant use until midnight.

Next morning the *Stern* reporter returned to continue his interview. He brought a gift – an elaborately decorated bow and arrow covered in gilt. He had the idea that Phoolan might pose for a photograph to illustrate his article. I should have liked to see her in action but two hours later she was still choosing her wardrobe. I went off to Shankar market to buy material for myself and be measured for a linen suit. I took some photographs of what I required, since men's fashions in Delhi lagged behind those in London. In general, and in contrast to Indian women, Indian men, apart from the young, dressed scruffily. An old tweed jacket or cardigan was their idea of Western chic. When I returned to Gulmohar Park it was to learn that Phoolan had taken Shiv Narayan to the railway station to catch the Gwalior train. However, they had set off too late and they both returned.

Later in the day, a friend of the family took me on one side. He told me that Channel 4 had sent Phoolan a new offer. He felt that she should seriously consider it, since the offer might soon be withdrawn and then C4 might just go ahead regardless with their legal battle. It was difficult for me to know if his advice was sincere or he had been put up to it. Nevertheless, I said that I would speak to her.

I managed to get hold of Baldev, the *Stern* reporter's translator, at his nearby residence. In the evening we spoke to Phoolan. She was still determined to prevent the Indian release of *Bandit Queen*. I told her frankly that, hard as we had tried to stop the film, we had failed. It had already been released in Britain and would soon be shown elsewhere in the world. As a consequence, pirated editions of the uncut film had already entered India and were selling briskly in Delhi markets for 400 rupees. Would it not, I suggested, be better for the censor-edited film to be released in Indian cinemas, so that most Indians would see that version? In addition, I pointed out to her that if she wanted money for her new organisation, or to go into politics, it would be better for her to have her own money, rather than become beholden to those who might demand something in return.

Phoolan said that the French publisher had told her that if she signed anything with Channel 4 then her contract with them would be cancelled. She suggested that I telephone Paris and see what I could find out.

I spoke to Susanna Lea at Laffont. She remembered me. She told me that she and their lawyers had been going through the latest Channel 4 offer and that it stank. They wanted to bind Phoolan for her lifetime to do another book or film for C4. This would effectively stop the publication of the book she had already written with Laffont. She assured me that if Phoolan stayed with them, then they would look after her for life. I believed her. Fortunately, Susanna was coming to Delhi the following week. She agreed with me that a meeting between herself, Channel 4 and Phoolan would be a sensible way to proceed. I checked this out with Phoolan and she agreed too.

When I put the phone down, I felt I had done all that I could usefully achieve. I could go off on my travels with a clear conscience. I of course did not know whether the C4 offer was as Susanna had portrayed, but the main thing was for there to be a compromise. I wondered if Channel 4 would accept one. I knew from my own dealings with them what bastards they could be.

*

I left on the 10 p.m. train to travel for a month. I visited Lucknow, Varanasi, Calcutta, Puri, Ajanta, Omkareshwar and Indore. Apart from seeing some wonderful places, I went to various institutions to see if there were any job opportunities. Most conservation departments were a shambles. In Varanasi and Calcutta, extremely valuable books and archives were being repaired with totally unsuitable materials. Those in charge were not interested in changing their ways. The only proficient facility I saw was at INTACH in Lucknow. Unfortunately, the director there had previously had a negative experience with expatriate conservators, who had imagined they were on some sort of holiday, and he was reluctant to consider employing me. It looked as though for the time being I would have to give up any idea of working in India.

My visit to Varanasi, supposedly the peaceful spiritual capital of the Hindus, somewhat confirmed the tales I had heard of the violence in eastern Uttar Pradesh. Wealthy landowning families from the surrounding countryside were hosting a number of large weddings. These presented an extraordinary spectacle. Long processions of smartly dressed guests were led through the streets by men on bicycles who played electric guitars or by bagpipers in full Highland regalia. Power for the guitars, and for the dozens of fluorescent tubes and strings of fairy lights, came from generators trundled alongside by oxen. Then came the landlords themselves, guarded by considerable armies of men with pistols, rifles and sub-machine guns. My visit to the conservation department of Banaras Hindu University was curtailed in the panic that ensued when assassins on motorbikes gunned down a member of staff on the campus.

While travelling, I read some Indian newspaper items about Phoolan. It was reported that she was too busy organising Eklavya Sena to get involved in politics, and that her autobiography in French was about to come out. On 12 March the *Sunday Times* announced that the *Bandit Queen* case had been settled. It reported that four scenes would be cut from the Indian version but none overseas. Channel 4 would give

Phoolan £40,000. This seemed a reasonable deal in the circumstances and would make her more independent. I hoped the French book would not be hindered. I tried to telephone Phoolan but could never get through.

Just before I returned to Delhi, *Sunday* magazine ran a major article on the *Bandit Queen* saga. A piece followed by Arundhati Roy. She had been one of Phoolan's main supporters in trying to block the film, at some cost to her own career as a scriptwriter, and I was sorry to learn that she had not been told in advance of the arrangements to settle. 'I spent a day feeling bewildered, stupid and let down.' However, she had soon come to terms with events – 'I don't consult Phoolan Devi about what I do with my life. Why should she consult me about hers?' She then went on to add – 'Given the circumstances, she has acted with intelligence and acumen. I've often said about her that it must be terribly frustrating to be clever – I'd say close to brilliant – and illiterate. It's a pity there's no sign of this in the film.' It was, I thought, a gracious tribute.

*

I arrived back at Delhi Nizamuddin railway station at 6 a.m. on 27 March. I would be leaving for London five days later. I cleaned up and had breakfast before going to Gulmohar Park. Phoolan and Umed were in bed. It seemed they had also just returned that morning, having been to a meeting at Bareilly, north of Agra. They had been accompanied back to Delhi by Phoolan's mother, Moola, who I had met very briefly in Gwalior in 1992, and also by Santosh, whom I had met in Delhi a year ago. Both seemed very glad to see me again. At 10 a.m. Phoolan appeared.

Phoolan looked strained. She was carrying a bank statement in Umed's name, which she asked me to examine. I discovered that in mid-March there was a credit for twelve lakhs

(1,200,000) rupees. She had been told nothing about this large amount and said that she would investigate. She took the statement back into the bedroom. A little while afterwards, Umed appeared. He greeted me in a very perfunctory way.

I went to the National Museum and met the head of conservation training. He was very sympathetic but doubted whether I could obtain employment in an Indian government organisation. This was the final blow to my prospects of working in India.

Next day, while Umed was out, Phoolan made a lot of secretive telephone calls. She needed someone to dial the numbers for her but was very adept at scrambling any memory afterwards so that the re-dial facility did not work. Eventually she told me that the twelve lakhs was money from the *Bandit Queen* people. Presumably it was for Umed's assistance in getting Phoolan to settle. I was appalled.*

'Don't worry,' she told me, 'I'll make sure I get it back!'

The twenty lakhs paid into court was already safely in her own account. She confirmed that the settlement allowed the publication of the French book. It would come out in August. Afterwards, there would be editions in other languages, including English.

*

My last few days in Delhi were marred by my breaking a front tooth as I bit into a roasted corn-on-the cob. Nevertheless, I managed to do quite a lot – I visited the Bahia 'Lotus Temple', the Lalika temple of the goddess Kali, the old Mughal fort of Purana Qila and the ancient tower of Qutb Minar. I also had a suit made and bought a lot of books, mostly novels of Indian life translated out of vernacular languages, to take home with me.

* Farrukh Dhondy, the commissioning editor of Channel 4, revealed that he had organised this payment in an article that he wrote for the *Asian Age* of 21 February 2002.

I went with Phoolan to the shrine of the Sufi saint Nizamuddin, where we put strings of roses on his tomb. Most of the devotees were Muslim but there were a significant number of others. We were all given blessed sweets to take home – the same ritual as at a Hindu shrine. I saw one or two people give us a strange look, but everyone was most friendly. Afterwards, as had become routine in the evenings, we went to the market for vegetables. Phoolan removed the covering she had put over her head at Nizamuddin, but no one recognised her.

At the flat, there were signs of the film money being spent. A large new fridge arrived. There were many visits by salesmen and the protracted purchase of a car. Umed did the bargaining, with Phoolan in the background making the decisions. The day before I left, an almost new white Contessa, a car similar to the British Vauxhall Victor, was finally bought. Before the first drive, Moola, Phoolan's mother, led a little ceremony to mark this milestone in the family's prosperity. A coconut was broken open and its milk sprinkled over roses strewn on the car's bonnet. Smouldering sticks of incense were inserted into the radiator grille. There were prayers for everyone's safety.

My last day in India was the first day of April. It was cele-brated with an odd mixture of Western and Indian customs, for in addition to it being April Fool's Day it was also New Year's Day for some Hindus. Lots of April Fool tricks were played. Most required the use of the telephone. One involved pretend-ing that Phoolan needed an immediate visa to go to Paris. To mark the New Year, the interior of the flat was washed clean and all the gods in the sitting-room shrine were carefully dusted, polished and decorated with flowers.

Phoolan went out in the afternoon. At 5 p.m., when I was due to leave for the airport, there was no sign of her. Very disappointed, I was just going out of the door when she returned. It was an emotional farewell. She made me promise that I would come back the following year.

5
Politics

'I looted those who looted you.'

FOR MUCH of the rest of 1995 I was preoccupied with my search for employment. My contract at Canterbury Cathedral Archives finished in the August. I had hoped to move to the National Archives. I was shortlisted but the post was withdrawn on the week of the interviews. Although I knew that I could always become a self-employed conservator again, that would take a considerable time to set up. Fortunately, the post of senior conservator at the huge Senate House Library of the University of London became vacant and I was appointed. I started there in the November. It would not have been politic for me to take any leave straight away, so I resigned myself to remaining in London until towards the end of 1996.

Meanwhile, Indian friends told me that it had been reported that Phoolan was estranged from Umed. She had said, I was told, that Umed had assaulted her. I found that hard to believe, especially as a bodyguard was always around. She also was reported as saying that he had tried to cheat her. That, I supposed, was the real reason for their break-up.

On my return to London I had written to Phoolan to thanks her for her hospitality. I had, perhaps rather presumptuously, also written:

> In my opinion, you will do best not to join any of the exist-
> ing political parties. It will be better to be independent, but to

offer some support to the politicians who most follow the ideas of Eklavya Sena. That way they will favour you, and you will not be associated with their corrupt behaviour. Also, that way, you can support different parties in different states if you want to. Later on, perhaps, you can become an independent MP or MLA. Of course, I am not really an expert in Indian politics, so you must do what you think best, and I will support you.

My advice seemed to have fallen on deaf ears. In May, *India Today* carried an article describing how surrendered Chambal Valley bandits were entering politics. Mohar Singh, who had faced charges for a hundred and fifteen murders, was campaigning for the Congress; Malkan Singh, another dacoit, was campaigning for a Congress breakaway party. 'Phoolan Devi did the predictable thing when she recently shared the dais with Janata Dal* leaders at a public meeting in the capital, making her intentions plain to all. Although she didn't stand up to deliver a speech, her presence was eloquent enough.' In July, it was reported that Janata Dal politicians were still trying to induct Phoolan into their party.

I heard very little from or about Phoolan for the rest of 1995. I wrote to her a couple of times. I received a letter from her, asking when I was coming to India. She had moved from the flat that the French publishers had provided, to one a couple of miles further east, in Chittaranjan Park.

*

The year 1996 started badly for Phoolan. On 24 January it was reported in *The Times* that *Bandit Queen* was about to open in Delhi. This led to a clamour from some of the upper-caste Thakurs to have her re-arrested. Rather bizarrely, Phoolan had been on stage the week before at the Indian Film Festival for the

* The People's Party, which had its origins in opposing the corruption and authoritarianism of the Congress government of Indira Gandhi.

première. The director, Shekhar Kapur, had left before the film as a protest against the cuts inflicted by the censors. Ominously, *The Times* article concluded – 'Thakur leaders say they will not rest until she is dead.'

In February I received a letter from Phoolan. It was written from Delhi, in poor English, and dated 27 January:

Dear Brother,

I have received your loving letter and I feel very happy that you have a job. Here all are very fine and hope same to you.

Many and often time I try to write you a letter but due to circumstances I couldn't write, for this I am very sorry.

This time I am writing you a letter when I am in trouble. You already know that I am already burden with lots of cases, but unfortunately again the old cases are all reopen and Supreme Court too ordered a NOTICE to give an attendance whenever they required. So these days I am absolutely dishearted.

Brother, you know I have full trust in 'DURGA MAA' as she has already save me in past, as she always save me in future too. You know well that SHE give me true decision and I have full faith.

I don't care about all these cases if Goddess will not help me then I don't fear about my death too. But what will be in future God knows well. It's my personal request that you don't dishearted because of my letter, you know how busy I am on these present days. Please excuse for all this.

You know Indian government didn't allow me to go outside India but I try to come anyhow, if ever I come to foreign country I never forget to visit you. It is also my personal request that you keep on writing letter because this is the way I know your health and affairs. These days I always remember you.

Don't worry about my cases it all depend upon God but from my side I had good and big advocate for the cases but all on faith.

Here we are all fine and hoping same for your family.
Whenever you come to India don't forget to visit me.

Here I too fine but due to cases I am quite disturbed. Please
give my regards to your mother and elders and youngsters too.
I received your photographs they are quite good.

Please reply me. Your Sister,

Phoolan Devi

It was difficult for me to know whether Phoolan's fears were
justified or not. It seemed unlikely that she would be given the
death sentence, but she might well be sent to prison for many
years. I doubted that she still had the mental resilience to
endure that.

A little later, it was reported that Phoolan was going to stand
for parliament. I wrote to wish her well. I continued:

These present ministers treat politics as a money making
business. It is time they were replaced.

But do remember too, sister, that all politics attracts crooks.
Even in the good political parties there are many liars and cheats.
People will promise anything to get power. Be on your guard.

Also, I pray, be careful of your personal safety. Keep your
security arrangements secret. Be very careful.

Do not worry too much about your old cases. It is possible
the court may take years to finally decide. However, there is
no way they can find you guilty. Remember that it was their
responsibility under the constitution to bring the case to court
when you surrendered. They did not do this, and cannot properly proceed all these years later. Even if they did, the evidence
would be too old to be reliable. Also the publicity would be
very bad for India in other countries.

I shall definitely be coming to India in October. You can be
sure I will visit you. I have written to your mother, to ask if I can
visit her at her village. It will be very interesting for me to see
village life. In England, people only know about life in Indian

towns but, as you know, most Indians live in small villages. I come from a small agricultural town myself, so it will be of special interest to me.

It was true that I wanted to see Indian village life. I had been brought up in the small town of Evesham in Worcestershire when its economy had been dominated by market-gardening. Many of our neighbours cultivated a few acres on the outskirts of the town and there were two large wholesale fruit and vegetable markets in the town centre. My own family was not in horticulture – my father, who died when I was ten, managed a bakery and my mother ran her own knitwear shop – but those of many of my school friends were. Most of them lived in the surrounding villages. Through them I was able to obtain casual jobs in the school holidays. I had harvested root vegetables and picked sprouts. Mostly, however, I had picked fruit. Evesham was famous for its plum orchards.

After leaving school, I had intended to study for a degree in agricultural chemistry. This involved spending a preliminary year in agriculture. I worked for a year on a fruit farm in Herefordshire, which also had livestock. There was trouble in my obtaining a grant to go to university and it was then that I decided to go off to an African tea estate. Subsequently I had marketed agricultural machinery and visited innumerable farms. After I returned to Britain in the 1970s, I kept up my links with Evesham and its horticulture. Neighbours of my mother had large fruit orchards. Every August I used to go there to camp out and pick fruit.

It was true, therefore, that I had a long-time interest in agriculture and country life. However, I was, of course, also very keen to see the village in which Phoolan had been reared. I had got on well with Moola, Phoolan's mother. She had suggested that I might visit.

*

There was an account in *The Times* of aggressive campaigning by Phoolan. 'I looted those who looted you,' she was reported to have told cheering Dalits and low-castes. 'I am one of you.' Meanwhile the upper-caste Thakurs had sent a 'widows' chariot', carrying twenty-two widows of the men from Behmai that Phoolan's gang was alleged to have murdered, to the constituency that Phoolan was contesting at Mirzapur.

This was the first time I had learned that Phoolan was seeking election from Mirzapur in Uttar Pradesh. It was the town between Allahabad and Varanasi that I had visited in 1992. It was well known for manufacturing beautiful carpets. There was a legend that several hundred years ago bandits near Mirzapur had attacked a camel caravan. The sole man to survive had been a Persian carpet-weaver. He had been given refuge and he had then taught his saviours how to weave fine carpets. It was now a considerable industry.

The *Times* article mentioned rumours that Phoolan was accepting money from the carpet bosses, who wanted to keep their circumvention of the child-labour laws hidden. This, if true, would be disturbing. However, it might well be that Phoolan was playing a complicated long-term political game. I had confidence in her. I remembered that it was from the temple near Mirzapur that I had bought the image of the goddess Vindhyavasini Devi to give to her in jail – a picture that she still displayed in her shrine at home. It seemed an extraordinary coincidence. I hoped that it would bring her luck.

On 19 April the *Asian Age* reported that fourteen widows of Behmai were that day to petition the Supreme Court to order Phoolan's immediate arrest. Their lawyer was quoted as saying: 'We want the honourable court to see the kind of injustice these people have suffered only because some of our politicians have chosen to glorify a criminal.' Next day it was reported that the Supreme Court had decided to hear the petition in July. This left Phoolan out on parole and able to continue campaigning.

Phoolan was seeking election as a member of the Samajwadi [socialist] Party. This was an offshoot of the Janata Dal, on whose platform Phoolan had appeared in 1995. Its leader, Mulayam Singh, was the former Chief Minister of Uttar Pradesh who had dropped the outstanding charges against Phoolan and facilitated her release from prison. A report in the *Daily Telegraph* suggested that Phoolan had become a formidable campaigner, with the Samajwadi Party 'wheeling her around most of the 85 constituencies of Uttar Pradesh, India's largest and most turbulent state.'

On 12 May I was listening to the BBC Radio 4 news, when they reported that Phoolan had won. She had a majority of 37,000. It was excellent news. However, I could not help thinking that she would now be so busy that I would see little of her when I went to India. I supposed that her victory would make it less likely that her parole would be cancelled. (Reports from India usually described Phoolan, after her release from jail, as being on parole. It seemed to me that since she had never been found guilty by a court, she was really out on bail pending a trial.) Perhaps the possible termination of her parole had been in Phoolan's mind when she decided to enter the dubious world of Indian politics.

When I saw the itemised Mirzapur results, I was amazed by the size of the electorate. It was one of the largest in India. The sixty-one candidates had received a total of 701,580 votes. (In the UK constituency in which I lived they were lucky to get 35,000 people to vote.) Phoolan had received nearly 300,000 votes. She now represented a huge number of people.

I wrote to Phoolan to congratulate her. I also sought to reassure her about her future:

> Durga is favouring you Phoolan, so do not worry about your case in the Supreme Court. Everything will turn out all right for you. You will remember when you were in jail in Gwalior, and

how you despaired that you would not be released. I told you
that your release would come soon, and I was right. Now, I am
telling you that Durga will protect you during this case.

As expected, the final results from the election gave the
right-wing Hindu nationalist party, the BJP, the most seats.
They were offered the opportunity to form a government but
after a few days this effort collapsed. A coalition of the second
largest party, Congress, together with most of the remaining
parties, then formed a left of centre administration with H. D.
Deve Gowda as Prime Minister. The leader of the Samajwadi
Party, Mulayam Singh, became Minister of Defence. This gave
Phoolan a very influential protector.

There was, as could have been expected, much hostile
comment about Phoolan's election to parliament. Some commentators focused on her 'criminal background', conveniently
forgetting that one-third of those recently elected from Uttar
Pradesh had police records. Others worried that her famously
expletive-laden language, which I knew she could modify to suit
the occasion, would mean that nothing she said in parliament
would be admissible in the official record of proceedings. How,
many asked, could Phoolan, who could neither read nor write,
be expected even to participate in parliamentary business?

Phoolan was not, however, the only illiterate to be elected.
The voters of Uttar Pradesh had also chosen Shobhawati Devi,
the widow of an assassinated candidate. From Bihar, Bhagwati
Devi, an illiterate former stone-crusher, which was among the
hardest and worst paid of jobs in India, had triumphed. In both
Uttar Pradesh and Bihar over half of all women were illiterate
and poor. It was, as liberal press commentators pointed out,
not unreasonable that a small number of MPs who had first-
hand knowledge of that reality should be elected to represent
their interests. It was heartening to read that when Phoolan
made her maiden speech in parliament, in which she

demanded that Mirzapur should be included with those poor areas receiving government help to establish industry, she had been 'heard with rapt attention and there was thumping of desks by all sections after she concluded her brief speech.'

There were a number of other newspaper reports about Phoolan's activities after the election. They were either sympathetic or not, depending on the source. For example, there was outrage from some quarters when Phoolan was supposed to have stopped a high-speed train that she was travelling on to greet well-wishers at some unscheduled stops. Phoolan's sympathisers countered that she had encouraged the driver to halt only for him to meet people who had gathered to greet him on his last day before retirement. There were also differing reports about a visit Phoolan made to Gwalior Jail to meet her old fellow-inmates and give them presents. She was denied entry. Some reports had her meekly accepting this, other that she tried to force her way in. It was difficult to unravel fact from fiction.

Some reports were less contentious. None disputed that a visit to Amritsar had been a success. She had laid a wreath at the Jallianwala Bagh, the garden where in 1919 the British had massacred hundreds of unarmed men, women and children. On a visit to the Golden Temple of the Sikhs she had been presented with a *siropa*, a cloth given as a mark of honour, by the temple authorities. She had then gone to the temple refectory and baked chapattis for distribution.

The report from Amritsar mentioned that Umed was travelling with her. It seemed that they were reconciled.

*

Phoolan's autobiography was published. Originally in French, the English translation was entitled *I, Phoolan Devi*. It had been dictated by Phoolan on to tape and then turned into readable prose by the editors at Laffont. Each finalised page had been read back to her in Hindi for her to append her signature.

The book read very much as she spoke. She was frank about the retribution she had meted out to some of those who had ill-treated her. Her gang had called on Putti Lal, her first husband. She described how Putti Lal, a man in his thirties, had refused to wait for his eleven-year-old bride to reach puberty. In order to have sex with her, he had opened her up with a knife.

Not realising that the gang that had come was commanded by Phoolan, he had referred to her 'as a real little whore'. Phoolan had then appeared. Her men had severely beaten Putti Lal. Then Phoolan herself had whipped him. Finally she had 'jumped on his serpent and crushed it'. Putti Lal had been taken naked and bloody through the village. He had been left unconscious at the roadside with a note: 'Warning – this is what happens to old men who marry young girls.'

Not all Phoolan's tormenters had faced retribution. There was a particularly graphic account of her being beaten and raped by the police at Kalpi, the town near her village. After beating her and stripping her naked in front of her father the police took her into another room:

> They put my hands under the legs of the chair, and one of them sat down on it. Some of the others stepped on my calves with their heavy boots.
>
> I couldn't say how many of them there were. They did not see my face and I didn't see their faces. My eyes were shut like stones. I was a stone.

It was too upsetting for me to read the book properly. I skimmed through it. It was clear to me, however, that these were real events, not the manufactured caste conflicts depicted in *Bandit Queen*.

*

In 1995 I had come across a footnote in an old book that described an extraordinarily long hedge, which in the nineteenth century the British had grown across India. This thorn hedge had been to control the movement of salt, on which there was a heavy tax. The story fascinated me. There was nothing about it in the standard histories of India but, by following up a reference in the footnote, I was eventually able to unearth some of the annual reports of the officials who had been responsible for it. In the middle of 1996, I found in one of these reports a very rough map of the hedge's route. It ran close to both Delhi and Agra, and through the middle of Uttar Pradesh. This line would, it seemed to me, be relatively easy to visit from Phoolan's village. I wrote to Phoolan's nephew, Santosh, who lived in Gwalior, to suggest that we might travel together to the village and look at the remains of the hedge. I also wrote to Phoolan to tell her of this and of my intention to spend October in India.

In mid-September, a fortnight before I was due to fly out, I found a map that seemed to give a more detailed plan of the route followed by the hedge. It appeared that it had run very close indeed to Jalaun, the main town of the district that Phoolan's village was situated in. This reinforced my determination to visit the village.

*

I flew out of London on 29 September and arrived in Delhi early the next morning. I took a taxi to Chittaranjan Park. This was a predominately Bengali-speaking enclave that had originally been established for refugees from the war that started when Bangladesh broke away from Pakistan. The housing was similar to that in Gulmohar Park, where Phoolan had lived before. The small block of four flats was freshly painted in white and pink. There were large balconies with ornamental wrought-iron grilles and potted plants. More potted greenery lined the pavement. As we drew up, I saw Moola, Phoolan's mother, up on the balcony of the first-floor flat. She called down for me to come up. I was effusively greeted by her, her eldest daughter, Rukhmani, her youngest daughter, Munni, Munni's husband, Hargobind, and various children. Phoolan was away.

I gathered that Phoolan and Umed had gone to Uttar Pradesh. Umed was standing for election to the Uttar Pradesh state assembly as the candidate for the Samajwadi Party in the eastern town of Pipraich. Phoolan had gone to support him and it was uncertain when she would return to Delhi. She now had a proper secretary, Mr F. M. Das, who was at the flat. He had good English, which was needed for much business in parliament. He was an excellent translator.

Phoolan actually had two flats, with her family living in the one on the first floor. There was little sign of money having been spent on luxuries. I was pleased to see that success in politics and with her book had not led to a radical change of lifestyle. Nevertheless, the money that had to be spent in acquiring such a property graphically illustrated the dual economy that existed in India. It had cost, I was told, thirty lakhs, about £54,000. With property booming, it was already worth fifty per cent more. In such a middle-class area of Delhi, this was typical. Yet the majority of Delhi's inhabitants earned about fifty rupees a day, which was less than £1. Indeed, members of parliament received a salary of only 4,000 rupees a month. This, presumably, was to keep them in sympathy with the majority of their constituents. Although they received free housing and travel it was not at all clear, or perhaps it was, how most of them had managed to acquire so much wealth. Phoolan, with the film and her book, had a transparent source of other income. With other politicians it was opaque.

The bottom flat was used as an office by F. M. Das and also to accommodate the two plainclothes policemen, normally three, who took it in turns to guard Phoolan. Das suggested that I check into the nearby hotel where he was lodging. Moola would not hear of it and I moved into a bedroom in the lower flat. Covering a large bed in another room, there was a six-foot-high mound of saris, still in their wrapping, that had been presented to Phoolan as she toured the country.

Phoolan would be allocated a free MP's house in the centre of New Delhi, eventually. This, however, could take a while. After Indian elections those that lost their seats were normally reluctant to vacate their houses. Often they would cling on for months, or even years, and finally only leave after they had been evicted through the courts.

I floated the idea that I might go to visit Phoolan and Umed in Pipraich but everyone was horrified at the idea. They told me it was too dangerous. Apparently the lead-up to the election had been full of violence. The main political parties had each established a private army. The Samajwadis had a 'Red Brigade', the Bahujan Samaj Party (the BSP) a 'Blue Brigade' and the Bharatiya Janata Party (the BJP) a 'Saffron Brigade'. These were staffed by unemployed youths who were trained to combat (and to conduct) various ploys to rig the poll results. Many of these unruly young men carried lathis, heavy bamboo staves used for fighting. There had been much intimidation. The biggest challenge for the armies would be during the vote. It was common to attempt 'booth-capturing' – forcibly taking over polling booths to fill in blank voting slips in favour of a particular candidate. I gathered that this happened frequently in Uttar Pradesh elections, particularly in the lawless east.

It was hot in Delhi and in the still air the pollution was terrible. I could feel the irritation in my lungs. Chittaranjan Park was, however, one of the more pleasant localities. The flats faced onto a large expanse of green. At dusk, I went through its floral gardens to the temple of the goddess Durga – the favourite god of the Bengalis. There were plenty of devotees but, unlike the mayhem at many other temples, the atmosphere was calm and contemplative. Later, I went with Hargobind on the back of his scooter to buy vegetables for our evening meal. After we had eaten, although it was still early, I was tired and went to bed. I had just gone into a deep sleep when I was shaken awake by a policeman. He wanted to collect his pistol. Amazingly, I had not noticed that it was hidden beneath my pillow.

Phoolan phoned early the next morning. It seemed that she was not immediately returning to Delhi. The police guards I had become friendly with again firmly vetoed any suggestion that I might go to Pipraich. So, rather than kick my heels in Delhi, I decided to travel to Rajasthan immediately and return to Delhi later. I went to New Delhi railway station to book a ticket for a train that left the following evening for Kota. From there, I went on to the nearby Shankar Market to order a made-to-measure suit. On the way I encountered a disturbance. Apparently, a bus had run over a woman and killed her. A crowd was attacking the bus. Passengers were desperately trying to escape. The bus-driver looked terrified. Police were beginning to arrive. My auto-rickshaw managed to squeeze past. When I returned half an hour later, having finalised my business with the tailor, the bus was a smouldering ruin. I had been wondering whether I might try driving a car in India. I dismissed the idea as total folly.

*

I took a train to Kota and travelled in Rajasthan for ten days. I much enjoyed visiting the forts and palaces of Kota, Bundi, Chittor, Udaipur and Mount Abu. As always, I found the Rajasthanis witty and amusing. Once again I was struck by how all the work was done by the women. Nearly all were illiterate. While the men loafed in cafes, the women did most of the work in the fields, on building sites and on road construction. In addition they had to do all the cooking and look after large families of children and the old. Nevertheless, they were heroically cheerful. Even in tattered saris they managed to look elegant.

While travelling, I read reports in the newspapers that Umed was fighting a losing battle in Pipraich. One of these articles, headlined 'Pouch king gives Bandit Queen's spouse tough time', predicted that an independent 'liquor baron' was almost certain to win, since he was giving out free plastic pouches of illegally brewed alcohol to those willing to vote for him. His father, who was standing in a neighbouring constituency, was employing the same tactics. The police had recently intercepted a lorry of theirs carrying seventeen thousand litres of illegal liquor. This seemed to have hardly dented their supplies. Moreover, their men had illegally tapped the mains electricity power lines into the constituency to give their supporters free electricity. Both men were standing as independent candidates. When local people were asked who would win the election, the reply was, 'Pouch Party will win!'

*

I returned from Rajasthan to Delhi on 12 October. When I reached Chittaranjan Park that afternoon, Phoolan and Umed were at home. Umed had indeed lost heavily to the liquor baron. Surprisingly, both he and Phoolan seemed quite unperturbed about the defeat. Moreover, the two of them seemed to be getting on well together. Phoolan had put on a bit more weight and her face was becoming rounder, but she looked in better health and more relaxed.

Phoolan and I talked about what had happened over the past year.

'What is it like, being an MP?' I asked.

'Busy,' she replied. 'Everyone seems to think that I can help them. Sometimes over the most trivial things – family disputes or getting a job. I do my best but don't let it take up all of my time. I want to bring hospitals, schools, electricity and clean water to the poor in the villages. To stop child marriage and to improve life for women.'

'Are you making any progress?'

'A little. It's difficult to achieve anything in parliament. Once they are elected, most MPs forget the promises they made during the election and devote themselves to making money. But there are a few of us trying to change things. We want a percentage of government jobs to be reserved for women. Especially for women from the backward castes.'

'Is that going to happen?'

'One day. We are fighting hard for it.'

I was pleased to see that Phoolan was sticking to her principles. I doubted that she ever had, or would, deviate from them. She was unlike me, who had over the years moved from right to left. My leftish friends loved to remind me of how in the 1959 election I had actually canvassed for the Conservative Party. Those days were, however, long past, and I wholeheartedly approved of Phoolan's agenda.

In the evening Phoolan suggested that I went with her to visit her lawyer. I was expecting this to be the lawyer that Phoolan had hired to fight the *Bandit Queen* case. I was stunned when we pulled up outside Kamini Jaiswal's office. Kamini had, of course, represented Mala Sen against her in that case. Nevertheless, I was very pleased to discover that Phoolan was back under her wing. Quashing the outstanding cases of murder was far more important than the *Bandit Queen* affair.

Kamini was very welcoming to us both. There seemed to be no lingering animosity. Phoolan presented Kamini with an expensive microwave oven. The Supreme Court was scheduled to hear her cases the following week. Kamini was not particularly optimistic that the charges would be immediately quashed and I gathered that the chances of that were fifty–fifty.

Unfortunately for Phoolan, the courts were having one of their periodic attempts to demonstrate that they were immune from political pressure. Probably the hearing would be adjourned.

I had arrived back in Delhi with the remnants of a bad cold. Phoolan was very solicitous. She took me to the house of a famous 'healer'. This woman had an extremely pleasant manner, which exuded calm and charisma. After we had been given snacks and pressurised into eating a number of huge Indian sweets, she checked my pulse and felt my forehead. She then went almost into a trance, repeating the name of various gods for a very long time. Before we left, we had to pose for a group photo. Next morning, to Phoolan's delight, I did feel better. I was pleased too. I was not convinced, however, that the healer had been solely responsible for my recovery.

My recovery might have had more to do with Umed taking me out for a drink. Phoolan did not allow alcohol to be consumed in the house, so Umed surreptitiously took a bottle from his stash of Johnnie Walker and we went out together, ostensibly for more snacks. This also enabled Umed to order some meat. After her short lapse from Hinduism into Buddhism, Phoolan had returned to a vegetarian diet. She forbade cooking meat in the house.

Phoolan talked excitedly of her visit to Paris. Now that she was in parliament she had finally managed to obtain a passport, and had recently travelled to France to promote her autobiography. She was impressed with the widespread affluence. She contrasted the cleanliness of the streets with that of India. She enthused about the fruit and vegetables. Most of all she had loved the French bread.

She wanted to return to France soon to promote her autobiography and also to travel to Germany, where the book had been a major hit. She was also intending to see a doctor in Paris. It seemed, not surprisingly given what had happened to her, that she still had major gynaecological problems.

'I'll visit London too,' she said. 'I wanted to come from Paris, but there was not enough time. Lots of people have been inviting me to stay with them, but I'll stay with you!'

I slept downstairs again, but this time I was not alone. The two flats had five usable rooms. One was for Phoolan and Umed; one for Munni and Hargobind and their two children. Then there was Moola. Umed's sister's husband had arrived. Rukhmani's daughter, Usha, had also come as had Shiv Narayan's wife, Shoba, with her two children and her brother. At least one policeman needed a bed. There was also Santosh, who was with a friend. Following my letters about a visit to the village and my desire to see the old customs hedge, Phoolan had summoned Santosh to Delhi. He was to travel with Moola and me to the village. Afterwards he would help me with my researches. Rather than let Santosh and his friend sleep on the floor, I invited them to join me in sleeping on my double bed. It was not my idea of comfort.

The most conspicuous new arrival was Jackie, a massive Great Dane dog, named after the Bollywood star Jackie Schroff. Phoolan and Umed were fond of him. Sometimes he would join Phoolan on the sofa, which was barely big enough for the two of them, and go to sleep with his huge head on her knees. However, because of his meat diet he was always fed downstairs, so he much preferred to spend his time with those of us in the lower flat.

There was no sign of tea or breakfast in the morning so I went for a stroll. I bought tea at a little stall opposite the nearby police station, where I was joined by a man who questioned me as to why I was in the area. I told him and then learnt that he was the district magistrate's security advisor. (In India, district magistrates, sometimes called collectors, have not only judicial responsibilities but are also the central government's chief executives. They wield considerable power.) I asked him about Phoolan's security. He assured me that they kept a close eye on anyone suspicious. Moreover, he said that her bodyguards were excellent men. This was reassuring.

It was quiet at the flats. The men played cards, while the women cooked and looked after the children. Phoolan had a number of visitors, but she simultaneously watched TV and gave them little attention. It was good to see her more relaxed. We finalised plans for me to go to the village and I would travel there with Moola and Santosh in a couple of days' time.

*

On the 15th, I was up at 5 a.m. It was good that I had set my alarm, since Santosh and Moola were still sleeping. We quickly gathered our things together. With difficulty, we managed to wake a driver sleeping in the back of his taxi and hired him to take us to New Delhi railway station. There was a minor panic when we found that the roads out of Chittaranjan Park were blocked by construction work for the forthcoming annual Durga festival. However, we just made it in time to board the 6.15 train to Kanpur.

The train was a luxury air-conditioned Shatabdi Express – a train used mostly by wealthy businessmen and their families. It was the first time Moola and Santosh had travelled in such luxury. Moola was the only woman in the long carriage who sat cross-legged on her seat. Nevertheless, she looked immensely dignified. The two of them looked on with bemusement as the brash passengers talked deliberately loudly into their mobile phones, then still rare and expensive. We received complimentary tea and snacks, which they enjoyed. Although Santosh was literate in Hindi, the free newspapers were of little interest to him as they were all in English.

Five hours later we were in the major Uttar Pradesh city of Kanpur. It was a depressing industrial sprawl of two million inhabitants. From Kanpur, Moola's village of Ghura ka Purva was about forty miles to the south-west. We took a train to Kalpi. This train was not luxurious. It had wooden seats, was deep in litter and very crowded. We had to wait for people to get off before we obtained seats. Despite the crush there was a constant stream of vendors selling tea and snacks. Numerous beggars forced their way through. Some were blind, others were transvestites. The transvestites received generous donations from people who feared that otherwise they might be cursed. Money was extracted from me by an outrageous mock flirtation accompanied by kissing noises.

Kalpi looked interesting, with its numerous temples and grand ruins, but I kept thinking of Phoolan in the police station being raped. Fortunately we were in a hurry, for we needed to reach the village by dusk. Moola kept reminding us that country travel at night was not safe. On our way to the bus station we had an altercation with a policeman who wanted to know why I, a European tourist, was with two villagers. When Moola pointed out that she was Phoolan's mother, he suddenly became very polite and I gathered that he had been hoping for a bribe. At the bus station there was no suitable bus. We decided to take a *tempo*, a fearsome-looking three-wheeler, with a nose that was raised up on the large diesel-powered front wheel. This gave the impression that it was liable to take-off. Ominously, it had scraped paintwork and numerous dents.

We were just about to climb in through its open sides when there was a shout from across the road. Someone had recognised Moola and we were being invited to take tea. I was reluctant, not wishing to miss our departure. No one took any notice of me and we were soon seated on the carpeted floor of a shop, drinking *chai*, the over-sweet, over-milky tea of India. Just as I was beginning to fear we would be left behind, samosas arrived. When I voiced my concerns, everyone laughed. It was gently pointed out that the driver was eating with us and that the *tempo* was owned by the shopkeeper.

When we finally left the shop, the *tempo* was packed. It might have comfortably seated five, but there were at least a dozen adults and several children. I was crammed into the front with the driver and two others; Moola was behind with the women and children; Santosh and a couple of youths were on the roof. It was amazing that the vehicle could still move. But move it did, and we chugged our way along the potholed tracks that crossed the open countryside. These plains had sustained large populations for many centuries. Everywhere was cultivated. There were thousands of small patches of vegetables, maize and sugarcane. Oxen ploughed. There were numerous hamlets made up of tiny thatched houses.

Gradually we dropped passengers off. The *tempo* became more comfortable, and faster. Finally we arrived at the end of the route, at the small village of Mangrol. We still had three miles further to go, and the light was rapidly fading. We were just about to set off on foot with our luggage, when a tractor, the only one in the village, returned from the fields. We hired his services for a few rupees.

The tiny village of Ghura ka Purva was in almost total darkness. We walked through dark lanes to the house. This was of rough brickwork and small. We climbed up to it through a small front yard, past a tethered water buffalo and goat, up a few steps and onto a small veranda. Phoolan's younger sister, Ramkali, together with her two children, was waiting to receive us. As I had read and been told, Ramkali was indeed rather beautiful. She had a more oval face than her sisters, together with a smooth flawless skin. She had large almond-shaped eyes. Most of all, though, it was her poise, the way that she carried herself. She knew that she was attractive.

There was no electricity in the house and we had to make do with paraffin lamps. There were two rooms, a kitchen and an interior yard. Since the whole house was a mere twenty feet square, these were all very small. The only cooking facility was a *chula* – a tiny hearth on the kitchen floor, which could only take one vessel at a time. Nevertheless, Ramkali had soon rustled up a substantial and tasty meal of vegetable dishes, dal and chapattis. We ate outside under a totally clear sky. The stars were incredibly bright and there was a vast milky way. We were tired and keen to sleep. The women and children went into the house. Santosh and I bedded down on the veranda. We were on charpoys – the ubiquitous village beds of woven webbing that I loathed, since they were never long enough for my legs. I was, however, soon in a deep sleep.

I awoke at 5 a.m., but as the air was cold, waited before I got up. There was no latrine. It was considered acceptable to urinate behind a bush in the adjacent field. It was not considered acceptable to defecate there. Santosh took me on a long hike across the fields to the bank of the River Yamuna. Santosh, like the other men we passed on the way, carried a small can of water for his ablutions. I, rather ashamedly, carried my toilet roll. It must have been three-quarters of a mile. It was, I thought, good that the village was not being polluted. I fervently hoped, however, that I would manage to avoid diarrhoea. There was no sign of women making similar journeys since, to avoid encountering the men, they had emptied themselves much earlier.

When we returned, we washed under the neighbourhood pump. We stripped down to that essential for travel in village India, our boxer shorts. Santosh and I took it in turns to work the pump-handle for each other. I then carefully changed into new clothes under a towel. A crowd of children watched me keenly.

We went on a tour of the village, which had about a hundred houses. The majority were similar to Moola's. Most were thatched; a few had tiles. Many were of brick; a few were of mud. A handful were plastered and a few were even connected to mains electricity. The dwellings were arranged in rows on either side of deeply rutted lanes of bare earth and each had an earthen forecourt for their cows, bullocks, water buffalo or goats. There was an occasional tree – a papaya, a mango or a custard apple. The dividing walls between the yards were usually plastered with hand-moulded cowpats. These, when dry, would be used as fuel for cooking. There was a primary and a secondary school. These, however, had no proper facilities, but were merely sheds with blackboards. I met the English teacher, but his English was entirely unintelligible to me. Maths, however, looked more promising. On one blackboard there was chalked the symbols πr^2.

The village was entirely Hindu. There was not, as had been relentlessly portrayed, any caste conflict. Apart from a Brahmin priest and his family, all of the villagers were low-caste fisher Mallahs. I did see one dejected man who appeared to have been ostracised. It was Maiyadin, Phoolan's cousin, who was also a Mallah. He was the man, Phoolan had asserted, who had appropriated her family's land and had been the source of all her early troubles. I was introduced to many of the other men. The women, however, remained in the background, often drawing their *ornis*, the headscarves of their saris, across their faces. Whenever any of the women bathed at the pump, they would drench themselves with buckets of water but always remained fully clothed.

At dusk, a couple of boatmen took Santosh and me for a row on the Yamuna. The river was a few hundred yards wide. In August, I was told, there had been an exceptional flood. It had made the river over a mile wide and its waters had come up to the edge of Moola's yard. Some houses had been badly damaged. Nevertheless, everyone had been delighted, since it had left behind a new and fertile deposit of silt.

'Look over there,' one of the boatmen said, as he pointed to a small indent in the riverbank. 'That's where the police hid themselves to ambush Phoolan.'

'Of course, we told her that they were waiting,' said the other with pride.

'Yes. And when the shooting began, she outgunned them!'

They both laughed.

*

Over the next week Santosh and I devoted a good deal of time to questioning the villagers about the old British customs hedge. Since it appeared that it had run close by, and that the much higher price of salt on their side of the barrier would have enraged their ancestors, I was expecting a rich store of memories. Perhaps even folksongs. In fact, no one had even heard of the hedge. We went into nearby villages that lay on the line of the hedge and drew a blank there too. I even hired a four-wheel-drive vehicle to follow the line that was on the map. To my intense disappointment, nothing resulted. I was mystified.

Everywhere I went, people proudly showed me places where Phoolan had hidden, or where she had ambushed the police. She had hidden in many fields and on many roofs. There was a small police post in the village. The officers were not popular since like many police in India they were only interested in making money. To achieve this they were often brutal. I already knew what had happened to Phoolan herself. I now discovered that all the family had suffered badly when Phoolan was a fugitive. Moola was incarcerated in the dreadful conditions of Kalpi Jail for four months. Ramkali was beaten. Shiv Narayan, then only five years old, was beaten and deprived of water. None of them betrayed her.

There was a small stone building outside the village. It was entirely plain and had a flat roof. Inside it was plain too, with what at first looked like a fireplace with black coals. However, a small black stone bull on one side revealed its true function. It was a shrine to Bhairon, the vengeful aspect of Lord Shiva, who was invoked to destroy enemies. It was, not surprisingly, Phoolan's favourite shrine. She had stayed here for a long time, mingled with some wandering sadhus, as she evaded the police.

Throughout my visit, the villagers were preoccupied with the annual celebrations in honour of Durga. There were evening concerts in a little yard. Musicians played harmonium, tabla and cymbals to accompany enthusiastic singing of hymns to the goddess. It was also the time when the winter grain crop was planted. A shrine in the concert yard housed wheat seed that was germinating. It was festooned with religious icons. A twenty-four-hour reading of the Ramayana, the ancient Hindu epic, was broadcast over a public-address system. It was impossible to sleep with the volume, and the horrendous feedback, that washed over every corner of the village.

Meanwhile, the villagers went on with their daily lives. Although historically the Mallah were associated with fishing and boating, most of their time nowadays was spent in cultivating their land. At the time of my visit, much of this was being ploughed. There were small patches of vegetables and sugar-cane, but most of the landscape was bare. White oxen were everywhere, yoked together in twos to pull single-furrow wooden ploughs. Or they dragged harrows, which were usually just a heavy log.

Moola looked after two plots of land of about two-and-a-half acres each. One of these was the land that had been seized by Maiyadin's family and which Phoolan had forced them to return. The plots were now in Phoolan's name, because her father had left them to her, but Moola had the income. However, ploughing was a male preserve, so Moola had to rely on a relative to plough the land for her in return for a share of the crop. It was to be sown with sorghum and wheat. She and Ramkali looked after their one water buffalo, its calf and a couple of goats. Buffaloes were worth more than cows, much as these were revered, since they gave double the amount of milk. This milk had a strong flavour, which took a while to get used to, but it made delicious creamy yoghurt. Although yields were generally much less than in the West, Ramkali was currently getting a relatively good eight litres of milk a day.

Apart from leading the oxen, nearly all agricultural work was done by the women. They kept down the weeds and harvested the crops. In addition they had to winnow and grind the grain, shell the pulses and cut fodder for the animals. They also, of course, looked after the children and did all the cooking. Washing clothes and carrying water from the village pumps were also physically demanding and time-consuming chores. The women went to bed late and rose early. I had seen a survey that calculated that the women of rural Uttar Pradesh were lucky to get five hours' sleep a night – even when pregnant. That seemed to be borne out by what I saw. Certainly that was Ramkali's regime. Her daughter, Nandani, was three and her son, Mohan, nine. Her husband, who had beaten her regularly, had gone. He sent no money for their maintenance. I tried to minimise any further burden I was placing on her. It was impossible in that society for me as a guest to actually do any real work. However, I insisted that we took the children on our sightseeing forays, so that at least she could get on unimpeded. It was no hardship for me since, like most children of India's poor, they were very deferential to their elders. Nandani was also very amusing.

Ramkali was able to sell the seasonal surplus of milk. Nevertheless, with two children to look after, she was desperately short of money. Without appearing to turn down her hospitality, I did what I could to pay for things. When I gave Ramkali a large note to buy some sugar, she came back from the local stall in tears. They had taken the change due to help clear her arrears. When I left the village, I gave her some money 'for the children'.

The health of the villagers was not good. Although they were careful about where they defecated, they bathed in a stream that came through other villages. Its waters looked dubious to me. Certainly, many of the villagers had dysentery. While I was there, Ramkali developed a fever. I assumed it was malaria and dosed her with chloroquine. She recovered and I was then besieged with requests for tablets. I sent Santosh to cycle into Kalpi to buy fresh supplies for me to distribute. There were no telephones in Ghura ka Purva so while he was in Kalpi, Santosh rang Phoolan. She was not feeling well. There was talk of her needing an operation to remove some tumours. It was time for me to return to Delhi. I could go from Kalpi to Jhansi, where I thought I might be able to survey the landscape from the hill-fort and see the line of the old hedge. From Jhansi it would be easy to catch a train back to Delhi.

The night before we left the village the Brahmin priest invited us for an evening meal. I was astounded, since in rural North India it was most unusual for Brahmins, let alone Brahmin priests, to invite the lower castes into their houses. (I remembered, however, that it was a Brahmin priest who had rescued Phoolan from more rape in Behmai. She often told the tale. After her escape, he had been doused in petrol by her assailants and burnt to death.) I went to the Brahmin's house with Santosh and Moola. The bearded and weathered priest and his wife were most hospitable. We had excellent vegetarian food. The two pretty teenaged daughters, modishly dressed in salwar kameez, waited on us. There was even some banter about one of them marrying Santosh. I took photographs of them all and promised to send copies from London.

*

Early next morning Santosh and I left Ghura ka Purva for Kalpi and Jhansi. Before we left, Moola, who would be staying on in the village, took us to the Bhairon shrine. She prayed to the deity for our safe journey and put ochre on our foreheads. I then said farewell to Ramkali and her children. It was an emotional parting. I will never forget my time in that village.

Santosh had persuaded four of his young friends to take us on their bicycles. He and I rode sidesaddle on two and our baggage was carried on the other two. It was a rough track for such heavy loads. Nevertheless, we arrived at Kalpi in plenty of time for the mid-morning train to Jhansi. It was crowded and dirty. A number of passengers had brought along goats and chickens. In the crush I was amazed to see a young woman reading Shakespeare's *Julius Caesar*. Moreover, when I asked her if she was studying it for college, she replied that she was a science student and was reading it for pleasure. She was a fan of Shakespeare and had seen videos of his plays. Once again, India had surprised me.

When we arrived in Jhansi, a scruffy city of half a million, there was low cloud and drizzle. This made it unlikely that we would see anything of the customs hedge. We telephoned Delhi to speak to Phoolan. She sounded low. She expected to be operated upon over the next couple of days. I decided to stay overnight in Jhansi, hoping the visibility would improve, and then return to Delhi that evening.

Next morning I climbed up to the fort on the hill that domi- nated the city. For a short period the weather cleared and I was able to survey the surrounding countryside. There was absolutely no sign of the customs hedge. It was a great disappointment.

On one of the ramparts of the massive fort there was a notice – 'Rani Jhansi jumped from this place on the horse back with her adopted son.' Further down there was a tableau to illustrate her exploits. The Rani had been widowed in 1853. Under the 'Doctrine of Lapse', a law that the British had enacted to allow them to grab more territory, her adopted son was not recog- nised as the new Raja. The British took over the state and pensioned off the Rani. During the uprising of 1857 the Rani gathered an army and captured the fort. Eventually it was retaken by British forces. The Rani escaped on horseback but 'dressed like a man . . . holding her sword two-handed and holding the reins of her horse in her teeth', died in battle at Gwalior. She had become a national heroine.

'For us from the lower castes,' Santosh remarked, as he studied the tableau, 'Phoolan is our very own Rani of Jhansi.'

It was a comment I would often hear repeated.

*

Santosh took a train to Gwalior, where his family needed him. He was disappointed that I was not going with him. I explained that I wanted to see what was happening to Phoolan. I did not mention to him that I was also thinking of proceeding from Delhi to the northern hills for a week on my own. Much as I had enjoyed my time in the village, it had been a strain to be under constant scrutiny. I had been such an unusual visitor that every little thing I did had been intently examined. I would often look up from merely applying sun-cream or adjusting my sandals to see that I was being watched. Because of the poor light inside the house, I had to shave in the open, and this would invariably draw a crowd of onlookers. It was tiring always being watched, trying not to make a mistake. I needed some time on my own.

*

My train arrived back in Delhi late that evening. At Chittaranjan Park, everyone was in bed. The place was choc-a-block with people but I managed to squeeze onto an already occupied mattress. Phoolan was in hospital. She was to be operated on in the morning.

At 9 a.m. I went with Shiv Narayan to the All India Institute of Medical Sciences. Umed was already there. Phoolan was in the operating theatre. We waited around, went off and came back. The doctors would not allow any of us to see her that day. However, they assured us that the operation had been a success.

Three days passed before I was allowed in to see Phoolan. She was surprisingly cheerful and showed me the three large bandages on her abdomen that covered the incisions. Her room was reasonably clean, although the ragged finish to the plaster-work made it difficult to keep it as clinically spotless as it should have been. No doubt she would have been receiving the best possible attention. Her recent visitors had not only included Mulayam Singh, the Defence Minister, and the Railways Minister, but also the Minister of Health.

Her breakfast arrived. She ate a little gruel, but gave me her eggs on toast. We talked about my visit to her village. She told me that in the early days when she was in prison her family had been so poor that she had been smuggling food out of the jail to feed them.

The day before this visit, when I came off a bus at New Delhi railway station, I had been robbed. Two men had pinioned my arms, while a third had cut off my money pouch. Fortunately most of my cash was back at the flat. However, my passport and air ticket had been stolen. The police had been awkward and would only give me a piece of paper to state that I had lost them. They flatly refused to accept that I had been robbed in their area.

'Of course not,' Phoolan said, with a wry smile. 'There is no way you could have been robbed in a place like that without the connivance of the police! The passport will be sold and they'll take a cut.'

She was, nevertheless, appalled that such a thing had happened to me. More appalled than me, in fact, for I expected the occasional incident when travelling. Worse things had happened to friends in London. In Morocco, when I had refused to buy some hashish, I had been seriously threatened with rape. In India a European traveller might occasionally be robbed but would very rarely be harmed. Phoolan wanted to give me the money for a new ticket but I assured her that I would obtain a free duplicate. Suddenly she seemed to tire and I left her to sleep. Even before I left the room her eyes had closed.

*

There were five days left before I was due to fly out of India. There was no question of my travelling north, since in order to check into a hotel I would have to produce my passport. In any case, I needed to spend most of the time that I was marooned in Delhi on the quest for a new passport and air ticket. Additionally, in order to be allowed to leave the country, I had to get an Indian visa. This was not easy, since many foreigners who had overstayed their visas pretended that their passports had been stolen in order to conceal the evidence. I finally received my visa on the very day that I was due to depart.

When I was not in queues, I explored the fascinating byways of Old Delhi. The weather had changed. The high humidity had dissipated and been replaced with fresher air. The pollution that had enveloped Delhi lifted. I enjoyed walking in south Delhi's numerous parks. I tried to spend as little time as possible at Chittaranjan Park since it was extremely crowded. Numerous visitors from Mirzapur and other places across India had come to visit Phoolan in hospital.

I visited Phoolan regularly. At first, it seemed she would soon be discharged. However, as the days went on it became clear it would take a while for her to heal properly. The consultant told me that Phoolan's Fallopian tubes had been septic. There were some lesions remaining that would need operating on at a later date. She was still in hospital on the day that I departed.

On my last visit to see Phoolan she presented me with a silver medallion of Lord Ganesh and the goddess Lakshmi.

'You must arrange to come to India when you retire,' she urged me once again. 'Come to live here and I will look after you.'

6
Courts

*'I will kill myself if I am not allowed
to lead a normal life.'*

AFTER MY RETURN from India in November 1996, I wrote to
Phoolan to thank her for everything. I also put in a plea for
something to be done to improve conditions in the village for
her mother and sister. There were all kinds of tensions within
the family and I did not want to interfere too clumsily. It was
obvious that Phoolan felt she owed more to her brother than to
the others. Maybe what had happened in the past justified this.
Nevertheless, despite their poverty, Phoolan's family in the
village had looked after me as best they could. I wrote:

> I wonder whether it might be a good idea for you to spend
> a little money on enlarging the house, and putting electricity
> in. Your mother is getting older, and she has had a hard life.
> Also you have to consider your prestige now you are an MP.
> In any case, the money would not be wasted, as it would
> increase the value of your property.

I had little news from India during the last two months of
1996. At the end of November there was an ominous piece in
the *Asian Age*. It reported that the Supreme Court had rejected
Phoolan's plea to quash the fifty-four cases of dacoity and
murder against her that were still outstanding. She would,

however, still be allowed to be free on parole until a competent court ordered her arrest. Which court was competent to do this was not clear. Phoolan's petition, also before the Supreme Court, that asked to have the case transferred from a district court in Uttar Pradesh to one in Madhya Pradesh was still undecided. I found these legal manoeuvres difficult to interpret and was not sure whether they favoured Phoolan or not. Meanwhile, however, Phoolan went into the New Year free to function as a member of parliament.

*

In January 1997 the Supreme Court refused to block an order from the Uttar Pradesh courts that sought Phoolan's arrest. A judge in Kanpur issued an arrest warrant in the Behmai case. This was under a law that had been enacted after the Behmai deaths that did not permit bail. It was an indication of the ponderous way that the law moved in India that he was the eighth judge to have taken over the Behmai case. His non-bailable warrant followed on from the previous hundred and ten bailable warrants for Phoolan's arrest. The authorities were ordered to bring Phoolan before the court on 4 February.

Alarmed at these developments, I telephoned Delhi. I spoke to Phoolan's niece, Usha, and also to a friend of Phoolan's who spoke good English. Phoolan was in hospital. When I expressed alarm, he assured me that Phoolan was actually in good health. She was in hospital not because she was ill, but in order to avoid being arrested.

There was a newspaper report that a projected tour of Phoolan to America and the UK in March had been cancelled. No one from Phoolan's side had mentioned this visit to me, so I was not sure if it had really been confirmed by Phoolan. She had been, the article said, due to address various British groups, including the Southall Black Sisters, the Newham

Asian Women's Association and the Oxford Women's Organisation, as well as several Dalit and Buddhist groups. It also reported that Dalits overseas had set up a Phoolan Devi International Defence Committee, with branches in Washington DC, New York, Chicago, Houston, Los Angeles, Hawaii and Canada.

On 4 February Phoolan failed to appear in the Kanpur court. The police said that they had issued a nationwide alert for her to be apprehended. They told the court: 'We raided her residences in Delhi but could not find her anywhere.' They added that they had spent five days searching for Phoolan in Delhi. They had been to her two homes and searched hospitals. 'We have sent messages to district superintendents of police throughout the country to arrest Phoolan Devi.' The judge ordered the police to produce her in court on 17 February. Outside the court, the lawyer for the widows of Behmai told the press: 'The administration is clearly trying to shield her from the law. She is covered under the X-category security and has four policemen guarding her. Then why is the police not able to trace her? Her guards should be suspended immediately for not informing their headquarters about her whereabouts despite having knowledge of the issuance of the warrant against her.'

In addition, the lawyer for the Behmai families was petitioning to have Phoolan declared by the court to be an 'absconder and fugitive from justice'. If this petition were granted all Phoolan's property and other assets would be seized.

I was taken aback by these developments. I realised once again that I was out of my depth in trying to interpret the Byzantine world of Indian politics and justice. The press in India had a field day. They were incandescent at what they saw as Phoolan making a mockery of the law. There were numerous editorials. The *Asian Age*'s was typical: 'The media may have invested her with a halo and written books and made films on her; she may have also won a Lok Sabha [lower house of parliament] election, but neither fact can give her licence to place herself before the law . . . she ought to be arrested.'

Not all the responses to the attempts to detain Phoolan were negative. The papers carried photographs of a demonstration outside the parliament buildings against her arrest. In front of a large crowd of sitting protesters sat Umed and Moola. Just behind them, gesticulating wildly, was Harphool Singh. Presumably he and Phoolan were now reconciled. Another photograph showed Umed, a heavy man, being dragged away by the police.

Phoolan's mother, Moola, was quoted as saying to a journalist who had enquired about her health: 'Son, forget my health. These upper-castes have made our lives a nightmare. My daughter has been running all her life. She has already served her imprisonment. I don't know why the court wants to imprison her again. We backwards are born to suffer in this country.'

On 17 February Phoolan failed to appear before the court in Kanpur. The exasperated judge issued a fresh non-bailable warrant and gave the police 'one more chance' to arrest and produce Phoolan. On 19 February he received an affidavit from Phoolan promising that she would surrender on 3 March.

On 24 February Phoolan made a sensational reappearance. She went to parliament. She was photographed, with a broad smile, next to the statue of Mahatma Gandhi. She told the press: 'I was not running away from appearing in court. I was in All India Institute of Medical Sciences the day the warrant was issued. I then went to Mumbai for medical treatment.' She also fixed a date to go to Kanpur – 'I respect the law. I will appear in court on 20 March.' That was the date that parliament would go into recess. Meanwhile, Phoolan was trying to promote legislation that would give half the seats in parliament to women, and inside that a quota for those from the lower castes.

I wrote to Phoolan, exuding a confidence I did not really have: 'Do not worry too much about your cases. I am sure that eventually all will be decided favourably for you. Trust in Durga Mata.' I was not the only Briton offering succour to Phoolan. There was outrage in some Indian circles when the Labour MP for Bow and Poplar, Mildred Gordon, nominated Phoolan for the Nobel Peace Prize. The British MP said that she saw Phoolan 'as a symbol of the struggle to remove caste, gender and class oppression from Indian society. The early part of her story – born into poverty, sold into virtual slavery, abused and repeatedly gang-raped while still a child – is sadly the everyday story of millions of the poor in contemporary India.'

Meanwhile there were developments in the politics of Uttar Pradesh that would cause difficulties for Phoolan. Since 1995, because of the inability of any of the political parties to form an administration in a hung assembly, the state been ruled by central government. This had enabled Mulayam Singh, Minister of Defence in the central government and leader of the Samajwadi Party, to exert influence on Phoolan's behalf. In March 1997, a majority was put together by the upper-caste BJP party and the lower-caste BSP party led by a Dalit, Kumari Mayawati. This bizarre coalition made Mayawati the Chief Minister of Uttar Pradesh. Mayawati was a great enemy of Phoolan. They had each accused the other of dividing the lower-caste vote. Phoolan, whose party had the support of most Muslims, saw Mayawati as selling out to an anti-Muslim BJP. Mayawati's appointment as Chief Minister greatly diminished Mulayam Singh's influence in Uttar Pradesh. Mayawati was now in control of the state's police.

It was Mulayam Singh who had originally arranged for all the cases against Phoolan in Uttar Pradesh to be dropped. Later, when this was deemed unlawful by the High Court, it was Mulayam Singh who had arranged for the state to petition the Supreme Court to reverse that judgement. The new Mayawati government had this petition withdrawn. The way now seemed clear for the state to bring Phoolan to trial.

On a more trivial note, but well illustrating the way life could become uncomfortable for Phoolan following the accession of the new government in Uttar Pradesh, the new administration was reported to have taken action against the premier club in Phoolan's constituency, the Mirzapur Club. This hundred and-ten-year-old club was used by wealthy carpet manufacturers. A new minister had phoned the club and asked who these men had supported in the elections. He was told that they had backed the Samajwadi Party and Phoolan Devi. Within hours the club, which was on a lease from government, was taken over and converted into an Uttar Pradesh government office.

Over the next six months there was a succession of hearings in various courts to determine whether or not Phoolan should be arrested and held in jail pending trial. At one stage Phoolan made an emotional speech in parliament threatening to commit suicide inside parliament if she was pursued in the courts – 'I will kill myself if I am not allowed to lead a normal life in society.' Another low-caste woman MP urged her on: 'Lift your rifle again. I will be with you.' Several times Phoolan's arrest seemed imminent – then the danger receded. Finally, in September, the Supreme Court ruled that the law under which the non-bailable arrest warrant had been issued could not be applied retrospectively in the Behmai case. This removed the immediate threat of Phoolan being returned to jail. She was, of course, still likely to be tried for those deaths.

My own inclination was to believe Phoolan when she denied being directly involved in the Behmai massacre. She had been frank in saying that she took men there to hunt for Sri Ram and Lala Ram, the two gang leaders who had killed her lover and then taken her to Behmai to be raped. She wanted to kill them. However, they were not at Behmai. She maintained that the villagers who had been shot had been killed without her autho-risation. Richard Shears and Isobelle Gidley had interviewed two survivors of the Behmai massacre for their book *Devi*.

These eyewitnesses, who had been presumed dead but had survived under the pile of corpses, were clear that Phoolan had not been directly involved in the shooting. This had been led by another dacoit leader, Ram Avtar. It was he, they said, who had shouted the order, 'Kill the fuckers!' I thought it unlikely that an unbiased assessment would ever be made. Least of all, given their record of delays, by the Indian courts. Meanwhile, I would continue to accept Phoolan's version. In any case, even if Phoolan had killed some of the men who had raped her, it would not have greatly disturbed me. Uttar Pradesh was not Worcestershire. In Uttar Pradesh, and many other places in India, the rich could buy immunity from justice. In an environment where the police and judiciary were corrupt, and where there was no law and order, a victim could be excused for delivering their own justice, if only to stop attacks on others.

*

While all these dramas had been going on in India, I had been pursuing my searches in London for accurate maps of the British customs line. I found a number of useful district maps in old gazetteers. Unfortunately, however, these had little detail since they were mostly on a scale of eight miles to one inch. At the Royal Geographical Society, however, I found what I had really been searching for. On a series of one inch to the mile maps dated 1879 there was a line of tree-like symbols clearly marked 'Old Customs Line'. The maps were highly detailed. Moreover, the sheets were edged with longitudes and latitudes. I bought a GPS navigator and taught myself to use it proficiently. I was confident that with the help of the maps and GPS, and with a good local guide, I could easily find the remnants of the old thorn hedge.

I booked my holidays for November and worked hard on my Hindi. I was well beyond the stage of merely being able to talk about the weather, but doubted whether I would ever be able to discuss complex issues with Phoolan or others. My trips to India were too short to make real progress. Moreover, I spent a good deal of my time in areas where Hindi was not the local language. In many Indian states the people, even if they knew Hindi, were reluctant to use it, as they feared Hindi hegemony. Many Indians preferred to use one of the numerous local languages or, if they knew it, English.

I wrote to Phoolan. I told her that I intended to fly into Delhi and that I looked forward to seeing her again. After sympathising with her over the continuing legal battles, I went on to tell her about my plans to search for the hedge. I suggested that if it was convenient for her, I could meet up with Santosh in Gwalior, or with someone else she could recommend, and then spend a few days looking for traces of the hedge in the area around Agra. I would then go off travelling in South India before I returned to Delhi to spend my last few days with her. She replied that she very much looked forward to my visit. She had spoken to Santosh and he would be happy to accompany me on my search.

*

I arrived in Delhi early in the morning of 1 November. I waited at the airport for a while, to clean up and have breakfast, before I went on to Chittaranjan Park. When I reached Phoolan's flat, however, it was deserted. I was completely taken aback. Normally, even if Phoolan was away, it was full of relatives and hangers-on. I was wondering what to do when a Sikh from the upper flat came out. He told me that Phoolan and her entourage had moved for the feast of Divali, which had started the day before, to her official house in Ashok Road, central New Delhi.

As it was still early, the roads were fairly empty and my taxi was soon speeding up the wide avenues of the Imperial city. Ashok Road was situated in the Lutyens Bungalow Zone of large Edwardian bungalows, designed by Sir Edward Lutyens for the high officials of the Raj. The white villa-like houses nestled inside huge wooded gardens. Sentry boxes protected the entrances to the residences of judges, generals and politicians. The Sikh had given me the wrong number and we cruised up and down, under the scrutiny of sentries and watchmen, looking for Phoolan's name board. Her house, No. 50, was unlabelled and we found it by accident when the policeman guarding the entrance recognised me.

Phoolan looked well and very pleased to see me. Umed was most welcoming too. Various other members of Phoolan's family greeted me – her mother, Moola; her sister Munni and husband Hargobind; and her niece, Usha. Even Jackie, the Great Dane, seemed glad to see me. Santosh, Phoolan's nephew and Usha's brother, was not there. He had gone to Gwalior as his mother, Rukhmani, was not well. I was found a bed on which to sleep until lunch.

After lunch we went to see a smallholding that Phoolan had acquired. This was about twelve miles out of Delhi, beyond the Yamuna River and inside Uttar Pradesh. It was a very fertile plot. Local women were harvesting radishes (the giant Indian variety that looked like a white carrot), aubergines and fenugreek. Phoolan happily wandered around, pointing out to me the virtues of 'home-grown' produce. The labourers seemed very fond of her. The women in charge took us to the little shed and made us tea. When we left, we were loaded with vegetables and sacks of millet.

We went from the smallholding to Chittaranjan Park. My impression that Phoolan was still very much a peasant was confirmed when we entered the upper flat. Most of the furniture had been moved out. It was filled with large metal cylinders that were being used to store the grain from Phoolan's harvest. Some of our party stayed behind in the lower flat and the rest of us returned to Ashok Road.

It had become clear to me that security had been stepped up since last year. There was always a plainclothes policeman around, with a pistol under his shirt. In addition another policeman with a light machine gun was always present. Everyone, including me, was frisked as they entered the premises. I chatted to one of the bodyguards and he told me that his previous assignment had been to guard Farooq Abdullah. As Farooq Abdullah was currently Chief Minister of Kashmir, and one of the most at-risk politicians in India, I was impressed. On the one hand, I thought, it was good that Phoolan's bodyguards were so well qualified; on the other hand, it was worrying that the authorities felt that she needed such enhanced protection.

It was the second day of Divali, the festival that celebrated the return of the god-king Ram to Ayodhya after he had defeated Ravana, the demon-king. This second day, I was told, was a special day for brothers and sisters. To my surprise, Phoolan insisted on honouring me. She put a tilak, a smear of ochre, on my forehead and then popped a huge sweet into my mouth.

I then, somehow, as was often the case, became confused as to what was happening. I had probably missed some hurried exchange in Hindi and so imagined that we were staying put for a late meal. Soon, however, I was being bundled into a station-wagon and we were heading towards south Delhi. We were going to a 'ring ceremony', when a prospective bride and groom exchanged rings prior to their wedding, of some relative of one of Phoolan's friends. I suddenly became aware that everyone else was dressed up while I was wearing sandals and an old sweater. When I protested everyone laughed.

The party was on the lawn of an up-market hotel. There were about two hundred guests, the men in smart suits and the women in expensive saris. Our arrival, complete with security officers, created a stir. Wide-eyed children rushed up to Phoolan to obtain her laborious autograph. The groom's father found us a table and gave each of us men a bottle of Johnnie

Walker 'Black Label' whisky, the most expensive brand in India. Our table was adjacent to a dais, on which sat the soon-to-be-married couple. They sat bolt upright on high-backed 'thrones', the young woman in a heavily embroidered sari, the nervous looking young man in a silk double-breasted suit. Later on, we clambered up to be introduced. A video team recorded everything for posterity.

On the way back to Ashok Road, having drunk more whisky than was wise in my tired state, I nodded off. As we reached the gates of the house, I woke with a start. It was 1 a.m. I was already clambering down to follow Umed, when Phoolan stopped me. We then headed off to north Delhi.

We stopped on the edge of a road near a large marquee. It was festooned in lights to celebrate Divali. Inside there was a large crowd of devotees, men on one side and women on the other, who sat on mats and were singing hymns. Facing them was an altar on which were flower-bedecked statues of Hindu gods and goddesses. Our host, who was a man I recognised from the engagement party, greeted Phoolan. He led her to the front, where she was garlanded with marigolds. I tried to remain at the back, but in vain. I was dragged forward and soon garlanded with flowers. Phoolan made a speech. To my embarrassment, she introduced me as 'my brother who helped me when I was in jail'. There was much applause. As we left, men rushed forward to shake me by the hand. One of the bodyguards whispered in my ear: 'You could make yourself a career in Indian politics!'

Back at Ashok Road I made up a bed on the front porch, took some paracetamol for a headache and, dog-tired, collapsed into a deep sleep.

*

Over the next couple of days Phoolan and I talked of what had happened to the two of us since we had last met. The threat to arrest her seemed to have receded and she seemed not to be too worried. Once again I marvelled about how she was able to put any troubles, events that would have crushed most people, behind her. She was optimistic and cheerful.

Phoolan talked of Mother Teresa's death and of how she had gone to Calcutta to file past the body. Actually, though, she was, like everyone else I met in India at that time, more interested in the death of Princess Diana. It seemed strange to me that a woman of her political leaning should be so concerned about a foreign princess. However, she insisted on hearing every little detail of what had happened. Later, on a visit to Old Delhi, I saw that on the stalls outside Delhi's main mosque, the biggest-selling posters were those of Saddam Hussein and Princess Diana.

Santosh returned to Delhi, bringing Moola with him. Phoolan had already told him of my plans and he was keen to help me in my further search for the hedge. Phoolan checked that I was happy with the arrangements and then went off by rail to speak at rallies in Agra and Jhansi. Next day, Santosh and I left by train for Agra. By good fortune, when Santosh and I arrived at Agra, Phoolan was waiting at the station to catch our train as it went on to Jhansi. There was a considerable crowd to see her off and the press took delight in photographing the two of us together. Phoolan introduced me to the couple she had been staying with in Agra, Madhu and S. P. Singh Baghel. They kindly urged Santosh and me to stay with them.

S. P. Singh Baghel was a leader of the Baghels, a shepherd community, which was one of the largest of the 'Other Backward Castes'. In his thirties, he had a cheerful open face and a classic Bollywood moustache. He lectured in defence studies at Agra College but was also deeply into politics. This he saw as a way of improving the lot of his mostly poor and uneducated caste.

Originally 'SP' had joined the Samajwadi Party, but when passed over as a candidate for the Uttar Pradesh legislative assembly had switched to Mayawati's BSP. He then became a MLA. Subsequently, however, Mayawati had appropriated some of the Baghel community's land for a park to commemorate the Dalit leader Dr Ambedkar. SP had resigned in protest. He was now looking for a seat in the national parliament. Since he was perceived as being capable of delivering the considerable Baghel vote to whichever party he joined, he was being courted by them all – not only the Samajwadis and the BSP but also the upper-caste BJP. It was a nice illustration of the complexities of Indian caste politics. What a leader might obtain for his caste was often more important than the party's ideology.

'Both Phoolan and I are in a strong position to bargain,' he told me. 'In Uttar Pradesh the upper castes and the Dalits are in the minority. Nearly two-thirds of the electorate are from the Other Backward Classes. My Baghel caste and Phoolan's Mallah caste together form a large part of the OBC vote.'

SP took me with him on visits to several outlying villages where there was a sizeable Baghel community. He was welcomed with garlands and was obviously highly regarded. We travelled in a four-wheel-drive vehicle, which was absolutely necessary as there were no proper roads. Most of the villages had no electricity, no dispensary and no clean water. The people were desperately poor. I sat uncomfortably on mats for hours as SP and the villagers weighed up what advantage they might get from giving their votes to one or other of the political parties. As we left each village I made a small donation to help purchase schoolbooks.

SP's life in Agra was very different. They had a small house in a leafy middle-class suburb. Madhu was from the Punjab and was an excellent cook. She was attractive and dynamic, and was in the process of opening a small beauty parlour. I imagined that it would do well. They had two small children, a girl and a boy. We went to sports day at the girl's school – very like sports days had been at my own school in Worcestershire, with silver trophies and the parents in their best outfits. We also visited the Taj Mahal and the tomb of the Emperor Akbar.

The main reason I was in Agra, of course, was to search for the old customs hedge. Since this involved wandering over people's land with maps and a GPS it was extremely useful to have the support of a local politician. Moreover, SP had a personable young nephew, Sachin, who was keen to accompany us. He knew the area and some of its families. We spent several days crisscrossing fields. The maps I had obtained from the Royal Geographical Society were surprisingly accurate. However, all the land where the hedge ran had been ploughed and cultivated. There was no sign at all of the customs barrier.

*

From Agra, Santosh and I backtracked forty miles north-west to Vrindavan. This small town was known as the birthplace of Lord Krishna and there were numerous temples to honour him – reputedly four thousand of them. It was the centre of the international Hare Krishna movement. We went on visits to their beautifully kept *gosalas*, cow hotels. I much enjoyed the sight of British devotees accompanying their chants of 'Hare-Krishna' with energetic 1970-style pogoing. The Hare Krishnas were immensely popular with the Indians.

We stayed with SP's sister, Pushpa. She also was active in politics and was a senior officer in the Samajwadi Party. She was an official in the Vrindavan branch of Eklavya Sena, which had five thousand members. I gathered that membership of this organisation of Phoolan's was expanding rapidly across India. There were even branches in Nepal and Pakistan.

'I've just come out of jail,' Pushpa told me. 'Mayawati had the police arrest me on a trumped-up charge. I was given a five-year sentence. Fortunately, Mulayam Singh was able to get the conviction quashed, so I was only inside for twenty days. Still, it wasn't pleasant.'

Once again, it was brought home to me how dangerous it was to be in Uttar Pradesh politics. She showed me her picture in the local newspaper. In it, she was smiling, but over her shoulder there was a double-barrelled shotgun.

Next day, Santosh and I took the train a hundred and twenty miles south to his home city of Gwalior. For me, it was just a brief visit to drop him off and meet his family before I departed for the south. Santosh lived in the police house of his brother, Mathura Prasad. This was the house I had gone to in 1992 when searching for Phoolan's brother. Normally Santosh's mother Rukhmani lived there but she had gone on a visit to the village. I met Santosh's two brothers. Shiv Narayan was out of town on police business but I had lunch with his wife and children. We also had time to visit various political allies of Phoolan.

The head of the local branch of Eklavya Sena invited me to her home. It was crowded with people. Many of them, I was told, were refugees fleeing upper-caste persecution. Somehow a letter I had written to Phoolan when she was in jail was produced and read out. This was greeted with great enthusiasm. The Eklavya Sena woman then tied a coloured cord round my wrist, put a tilak on my forehead and proclaimed me 'her brother'.

*

I left for Bangalore that evening. The first ten days of my visit had been interesting and exciting, but tiring. I still found it a strain to always be on display and closely observed. Now I was able to relax. After Bangalore I went to Udipi, Hampi and Hyderabad – all towns with a wonderful cultural heritage. I met up with a few old friends and made some new ones. The people in the south of India were, in general, much less demanding than those in the north. On the way back to Delhi, I broke my journey at Jhansi and Orcha to make another search for the customs hedge. This again ended in disappointment.

*

I returned to Delhi on the evening of 26 November. It was late when I arrived at Chittaranjan Park and I had to wake people up to let me in. A bed was made up for me on the living-room floor.

Phoolan woke me when she got up at 7 a.m. It was unusually early for her, but she was going off to meet a group of Sikhs in the Punjab. Despite my protests, she only found time for a small cup of tea before she left. I also protested when she put a large wad of chewing tobacco into her mouth. She smiled back at me. She knew it was not good for her, but she could not break the habit. She did not return until late evening. All the other women had for some reason gone off to Gwalior or the village. Since Phoolan still resolutely refused to have servants, she cooked us a basic meal of chapattis and a few vegetables.

Next morning, Phoolan had another hurried 'breakfast' before she drove off to meetings in Haryana state. When I complained that I was leaving that evening and that she was working too hard, she raised her arms in a hopeless gesture and said, 'Politics!'

That afternoon there was a bizarre episode. A young Muslim man came to the flat. A crowd of press reporters and photographers accompanied him. Earlier in the day he had climbed the main post office transmission tower and threatened that if no one helped him he would jump off. He was from Varanasi and said that he had married a Hindu girl. The girl's family had then kidnapped their daughter and locked her up. The authorities in Varanasi had refused to help. He had come to Delhi to petition ministers, but after a week of trying he had got nowhere. While he was up the tower threatening suicide, someone had shouted up to him that Phoolan might help. He had agreed to come down if Phoolan would agree to assist him.

Phoolan, of course, was in Haryana and it proved impossible to get hold of her. Her husband, Umed, had gone to reassure the man that Phoolan would help. The man had then climbed down the tower and been brought back to the flat. He was in his mid-twenties, well educated, with good English, and had his own textile business. Umed was very good with him and even managed to get a smile with a few of his jokes. The police were surprisingly sympathetic too.

Phoolan returned in the late evening. She listened to the young man's tale and told him that he could stay the night. She then phoned Varanasi and spoke to the girl's parents. I gathered that she was threatening them with dire consequences if they did not release their daughter. She told them she would be sending round some of her people to interview the girl, ascertain her wishes, and sort the matter out. The parents, alarmed by Phoolan's intervention, quickly agreed.

Simultaneously with this drama, there was a political drama being played out on the television. There was a crisis in the ruling coalition. The Prime Minister, I. K. Gujral, who had no clear majority, relied on support from Congress to keep in power. A commission had just implicated one of the coalition parties from Tamil Nadu, the DMK, in tacitly supporting the group that in 1991 had assassinated the Congress's Prime Minister, Rajiv Gandhi. Congress had demanded the expulsion of the DMK ministers from the government. Gujral had refused to do this. For much of November there had been negotiations. Finally the Congress had withdrawn its support for the coalition government and Gujral resigned

It now seemed that the coalition would be unable to put together a new administration. Elections were expected early in the New Year and the right-wing Hindu nationalist party, the

BJP, was gaining support. Phoolan might well lose her position as an MP. Mulayam Singh, her protector, might well lose office. These developments made Phoolan's arrest, trial and imprisonment much more likely.

I needed to depart at midnight. With all this ominous news coming through on the TV, and her fellow politicians continually on the phone to her, Phoolan and I had little time to talk. She was, however, keen for me to return next year. I assured her I would try my best.

'I really hope,' I told her, 'that before my next visit the cases against you are finally quashed. Good luck in the coming election.'

'Don't worry about me.' She gave me a wry smile. 'I'll be all right.'

There was just enough time left for a few group photographs before her driver whisked me off to the airport.

*

The year 1998 started badly for Phoolan. In mid-January there were reports that Umed had joined a rival political party. When questioned about this, she was quoted as saying: 'What do you mean by talking of that creep? He dumped me and wanted to use my name for his political gains. I have now disowned him and have nothing to do with him.'

With all her other problems, I thought, the last thing that she needed was a very public marital break-up.

There were various attempts by her political rivals to have her barred from contesting the forthcoming national elections. They suggested to the Election Commission that since she was out of jail only on parole, she was not eligible. The commission finally decided in Phoolan's favour.

It was, however, becoming clear that the upper-caste BJP was in the ascendant. All the national opinion polls predicted that they would win. Voting took place across India on 16, 22 and 28 February – spread out as usual to enable police and army to move around the country to keep order. The BJP did win the largest number of seats but without an overall majority. It put together a coalition with a small majority. The BJP leader, Atal Bihari Vajpayee, became Prime Minister.

In Mirzapur, Phoolan lost heavily. She amassed nearly 300,000 votes but the BJP candidate was credited with over 50,000 more. There were numerous reports of irregularities. It was alleged that BJP ministers in the state had used their department's official vehicles to transport BJP voters. Moreover, Phoolan protested to the Election Commission that BJP workers had blocked her supporters from voting in at least a hundred polling booths. Nevertheless, the result was allowed to stand. Phoolan was no longer an MP. Her position seemed precarious. The newspapers predicted that her parole was now likely to be cancelled.

Matters escalated in August. A court in Uttar Pradesh issued a non-bailable warrant for Phoolan's arrest in connection with two murders in that state in 1980. Once again she managed to disappear from view until the Supreme Court suspended the warrant. As always, Phoolan and her lawyers were determined to resist any attempt by the Uttar Pradesh government to gain control over her. She had originally surrendered in Madhya Pradesh in order to avoid that happening. She had always feared that if she fell into their clutches the Uttar Pradesh authorities would somehow engineer her assassination by the police. Probably they would pretend that she had tried to escape from custody. This had happened to plenty of others.

*

While all these dramas were taking place, there was little I could do to help Phoolan. She now had sufficient money from the film and her book to employ the best lawyers. All I could do was to write occasionally to offer my support.

I was busy with my work in the university library, but I found some time to continue my researches into 'The Great Hedge of India', as I had begun to call it. I had gradually become aware of the damage caused to the health of the Indians by the oppressive Salt Tax. In the evenings, I researched the probable physiological effects of salt deficiency; on Saturdays, I searched libraries for more maps of the Imperial Customs Line. I intended to go to India in the autumn to make one last effort to find some remains of the massive hedge. This, I decided, would be a last attempt – I could not spend the rest of my life searching for something that might well have totally disappeared.

I wrote to Phoolan to arrange a visit in November. I proposed to fly into Delhi but only spend one night there before going south and travelling for a while. Later, I would return to Gwalior to join up with Santosh to search for the hedge. Finally, before returning to London, I would come back to Delhi for a few days to stay with Phoolan.

*

My plane landed in Delhi early on 2 December. I did some shopping before going on to Chittaranjan Park. Phoolan, absolutely delighted to see me, looked well. To my utter amazement, Umed was there too. I gathered that after some months of hostility following the election fiasco, Phoolan had visited him when he was sick and that they had become reconciled. The only other members of the family in residence were Phoolan's sister, Munni, with her husband and their two children. The rest of the family was in Gwalior or Ghura ka Purva. There was a police bodyguard, since although Phoolan was no longer an MP, the Supreme Court had agreed to continue her protection. Sarfraaz, a very helpful young man from Lucknow doing a business degree at Delhi University, was also living there. He was a Muslim who assisted Phoolan in her many dealings with that community and more generally. His excellent English was useful to Phoolan, as it was to me.

We talked about the election Phoolan had lost in Mirzapur. It had been, she told me, a question of 'manpower'. Volunteers had been needed to get the vote out and to guard the polling booths. Some of the people who had helped Phoolan in the previous election had been recruited by Umed, and then moved with him when he defected. With too few helpers she had been unable to arrange effective security. Not only had many of her supporters been barred from voting when they arrived at polling booths, but masses of completed ballot forms had been seized and 'thrown in the river'.

Much of the talk in the house revolved around the extraordinarily high price of onions and the national shortage of salt. These were both politically charged issues and expected to influence the elections about to be held in a number of the states. Following exceptionally heavy rains and flooding, the price of onions had increased five-fold. The onion had a special place in the Indian imagination. Despite being denounced by some ascetics as a stimulant, it was regarded as an essential in the budget of the poor. Mrs Gandhi, in one election, had famously garlanded herself with onions to draw attention to the high price at the time. The price of onions often featured in the rhetoric of politicians. The government was desperately trying to find onions that it could import.

The shortage of salt had its origins in a cyclone that had hit the coast of Gujarat in June. This had raged over the saltpans that produced most of India's salt. It was estimated that some fourteen thousand labourers had been swept away. In fact, the labourers had soon been replaced from the bottomless pit of Indian poor. The salt warehouses had soon been restocked. There had always been enough salt for everyone and politicians appeared on TV in front of innumerable sacks. Nevertheless, rumour had caused panic-buying and hoarding. In Delhi the price of salt had escalated from five rupees a kilogram to twenty. In Bihar it had reached sixty rupees. There had been riots in several towns. Shops were looted. Onions and salt dominated the news.

The weather in Delhi was perfect – dry, with low humidity and pleasantly warm. However, we were getting close to winter, when it might go down to 7 degrees centigrade, and I knew Phoolan hated the cold. Moreover, she still had various abdominal problems. Heat seemed to ease the pain and in the evening she lay down on the sofa with a hot-water bottle on her stomach. I had brought a padded Alpine vest for her to wear. She loved it.

I also gave her a travel pouch that hung round her neck to keep her passport safe. There had been great embarrassment earlier in the year when her passport, which had taken her so much effort through the courts to obtain, had been stolen at an election rally. The press had a field day with this story of the 'Bandit Queen' being herself robbed. She had eventually managed to replace the passport and had recently gone to Malaysia. In December she intended to go to Japan, where her autobiography was selling well.

Sarfraaz and I slept in the lower flat. In London I tended to awake at the slightest noise but in India, as I had noticed before, I slept well in the noisiest situations. Sarfraaz chatted to visiting friends and the police security officers; the television was loud; the telephone constantly rang; occasionally, Jackie would give a booming bark. I slept deeply.

Next morning I went to the nearby Kali temple and prayed for the success of my forthcoming travels, then packed. Phoolan was packing too. She was off to campaign for the Samajwadi Party's candidates in the Madhya Pradesh state election. She intended to return to Delhi for the last week of the month. This suited me well, as I also intended to return to Delhi then. Phoolan phoned for an auto-rickshaw for me to go to Nizamuddin station and waved me off as I went to catch the train to Hyderabad.

*

My main reason for going to Hyderabad, a thousand miles south of Delhi, was to visit the National Remote Sensing Agency. I wanted to ascertain whether it was possible to obtain images from their space cameras that might show the route of the old Imperial Customs Line. It turned out that the picture resolution was insufficient. Nevertheless, the visit was a success – I had a good friend there, with whom I stayed, and the city and its surrounds were full of interest. From Hyderabad I travelled to Bithur, in Uttar Pradesh, a small town on the River Ganges.

This was my seventh visit to India. I had gradually begun to think that I should find a base – a town where I could find a house to rent, where people were welcoming and where I could integrate into the local community. I had drawn up a list of criteria. I fancied a small historic town, set in countryside and perhaps on an unpolluted river. It must be reasonably accessible. As I was learning Hindi, ideally it would be in one of the Hindi-speaking states. Moreover, in those areas Phoolan had influence and might be able to help me. Nowhere I had yet visited had seemed very suitable, except possibly Omkareshwar, so it would have to be somewhere new. I had spent many hours in London poring over possibilities. I had decided to investigate Chitrakut and Bithur.

First I went to Bithur, a small town full of history. It had boasted the palace of the last Peshwa to rule the Maratha Empire. However, when I arrived, I found that this had been destroyed by the British in the 'Mutiny' of 1857. That year, many of the other old buildings had been severely damaged. The whole town seemed dilapidated. There were no restaurants or hotels, not even a pilgrims' hostel. A Hindu priest rented me a bare room, furnished with a single charpoy. The ghats of weathered stone that stepped down to the river were attractive and I was fascinated to see swarms of moustachioed catfish coming to be fed. I chatted to the dope-smoking men who gathered there in the evenings. They, like everyone in Bithur, were very friendly and urged me to come and live. However, the air of decay that enveloped the town put me off, so I left for Chitrakut.

At first sight, I fell in love with Chitrakut. This was the town in the Ramayana epic where the god-prince Ram, the king's eldest son, and his wife Sita had lived after they had been expelled from Ayodhya through the machinations of the king's youngest wife, who had wanted her own son to succeed to the throne. In the Ramayana it was set in an idyllic forest, full of animals and birds. Now it was much the same, for most of the surrounding area was controlled by the Forest Department. The town was very small, dominated by pretty temples running along the little river. This river, unusually for India, was beautifully clean and full of fish. I lodged in a small hotel overlooking the ghats and watched bands of pilgrims going to bathe. This regular stream of pilgrims had led to the provision of more in the way of food and supplies than the town could otherwise have offered. It also meant that trains stopped at the nearby station, which had a daily direct service to Delhi.

I hired a boat and was rowed a couple of miles to the pool where Sita was reputed to have bathed. Every few minutes I would see the brilliant blue flash of a kingfisher. The boatman was a Mallah. He told me that all the many boatmen were Mallah too, of the same small caste as Phoolan. When I casually mentioned her name, he told me that he greatly admired her. Chitrakut, I thought, might be the perfect place for me.

I went from Chitrakut to Gwalior, where I met up with Santosh and most of the rest of Phoolan's family. I spent the night in the overcrowded police house of Mathura Prasad, Santosh's elder brother. Its two small rooms accommodated Mathura and his wife and two children, his brother and sister, Santosh and his mother. I was given a narrow bed while most slept on the floor. It did not seem that Phoolan's money had much changed their lives. Phoolan's brother, Shiv Narayan, who also lived in Gwalior, had received help to build a new house. It seemed unfair, but no doubt the difference was rooted in the family's past history. I assumed that Shiv Narayan was the favourite because he had been the one to support Phoolan most in the difficult years. It was a subject I avoided, happy to be friendly with all of them.

Next day, Santosh and I left for Etawah District on our final search for the remains of the customs hedge. We spent a week looking at various places where the line of the hedge and that of the modern road, which might have obliterated it, had diverged. We had to be careful since we were in bandit country, so we only travelled by daylight. It was the very same landscape of ravines from which Phoolan had operated so successfully. The driver of our horse-drawn trap regaled us with horrific tales of robbery and murder. We expressed suitable astonishment. Finally, we walked along the bank of the Chambal River to a small village where we at last found some remnant of the 'Great Hedge of India'. Although this was merely a few thorn-trees on top of an embankment, it was a great moment for us both.

I left Santosh in Gwalior and went on to Indore and Omkareshwar. I had been to Omkareshwar in 1995 and it was another of the attractive small places I had thought of as a possible place to live. It certainly met most of my criteria – it was on River Narmada, in the middle of the which there was a templed island roughly in the shape of the Sanskrit symbol for

Om: ॐ. This drew numerous pilgrims. The surrounding countryside was green and attractive. When I talked to local people, however, they were concerned about a huge dam that it was expected would be built very close. This made me all the more sure that Chitrakut should be my first choice.

From Chitrakut I went to Sambhar Salt Lake in Rajasthan to see the source of much of the salt that had been smuggled through the Imperial Customs Line. From Sambhar I proceeded to Delhi.

*

I arrived back in Delhi on 27 November. It was later than I had planned and it would only give me three days before I departed for London. Phoolan had been delayed too, but she arrived back from Calcutta that very evening. She looked happy. She was carrying a huge earthenware pot full of some special yoghurt. Also she had brought huge quantities of Bengali sweets, which the entire household fell upon with joy.

I told Phoolan about my visit to Chitrakut.

'I might look for somewhere to rent.'

'You should buy a place there,' she enthused. 'I'll give you the money.'

'No, no,' I protested. 'I can't let you do that. What do you think a house would cost?'

'Don't worry about the price. I'll come to Chitrakut with you, and bargain on your behalf. No one in India will obtain a better price than me! We should easily be able to find a house for two lakhs.'

Two lakhs, 200,000 rupees, was then about £3,000, which I could certainly manage. I knew, however, there were severe restriction on foreigners buying property.

'Don't worry,' Phoolan said. 'In India everything can be fixed if you have money. There's a lawyer nearby who deals with property matters. Go and see him tomorrow.'

Next day, I followed Phoolan's advice and went to see the lawyer. As Phoolan had suggested, there were ways around the restrictions. The river through Chitrakut was the boundary between Uttar Pradesh and Madhya Pradesh, with half the town in each state. Property law was different in every state, so nothing could be formulated until I had found a specific property. Then, the lawyer told me, he would be able to advise me how to proceed.

Until Phoolan had suggested otherwise, I had intended merely to rent a property. However, with her on my side, it seemed foolish to pass up the chance of buying a property at a bargain price. I began to dream of owning my own house in Chitrakut.

We all went on an expedition to look at Phoolan's small-holding. The drive, which took us across the Yamuna River into Uttar Pradesh, was not enjoyable, since we had to overtake numerous lorries on the poor road. We were constantly enveloped in clouds of thick dust. Our driver sped on regard-less. As I used to tell friends in Britain, who worried about me dying from disease or snakebite: 'If I die in India it will be in a road accident!'

Her land, like that of others in North India, had been flooded earlier in the year and she had lost the entire crop. Now, however, all was flourishing – fields of wheat and rice; vegetable patches with cauliflower, spinach, carrots, radishes and fenu-greek. The labourers, all women, were extremely cheerful and chatty. They brought us apples and lengths of sugarcane to nibble. Phoolan was in her element as she explained her farming methods to me. I told her about the market gardens in Worcestershire. We happily made comparisons.

Next day, Phoolan asked me to go through a disorderly file of royalty payments for her autobiography. Even though Phoolan was in very different circumstances to those when I had first contacted her, she still seemed to value my advice. She trusted me more than the sycophants who flocked to her. In India it was quite usual for someone to acquire a guru and then continue to consult them even after, to an outside observer, the pupil had overtaken the teacher. It seemed that I was in that favoured position, which I was happy to occupy.

It seemed to me that the French publisher, Robert Laffont, had done well by her. The book had been translated into most European languages as well as Malay and Japanese. Given that it had taken a lot of effort for the publisher to turn her verbal memories into text, and that in addition they had paid for her accommodation for a year while this was being done, the percentage she was receiving seemed fair. So far she had been paid $70,000. Much of that, I gathered, had gone to the lawyers for keeping her out of jail.

I left Delhi for London on the last day of November. Phoolan and I made plans for my return next year.

'We'll travel to Chitrakut together,' she said as I left. 'Perhaps we can also visit some other temple towns. I should be an MP again by then.' She gave a happy smile. 'This government cannot last. There will be another election soon.'

'Will you stick with the Mirzapur constituency?'

'Oh, yes. In reality I won last time. I'm off to visit there next week. With more manpower I'm sure I can triumph again.'

'And your court cases?'

'I have faith that the Goddess Durga will protect me.'

7
Chitrakut

Chirakuta, Peak of Beauty, where the forest
*   creatures stray,*
And in every bush and thicket herds of lightsome
*   monkeys play.*

*   From the Ramaya of Valmiki, translated by R. C. Dutt*

I RECEIVED a fulsome card from Phoolan for New Year 1999.
It had been written in English for her by Sarfraaz, who had
appended a greeting of his own. Phoolan referred to the letter
that I had sent after my last visit to India:

> I think you know what relationship we have. You are my
> brother! Therefore it is my duty to look after everything for you.
> It is not a matter of 'thank you for your hospitality' or anything
> like that. I feel happy to serve you the best way I can, and hope
> to continue for the rest of my life. . . . I will be very pleased if you
> go ahead for the plot in Chitrakut. I will definitely accompany
> you.

I was extremely busy in my spare time for most of the
year as I tried to finish writing *The Great Hedge of India*.
Nevertheless, I also found some time to follow in the media
what was happening in Indian politics.

In April the BJP coalition government lost a no-confidence
vote. The Congress politicians failed to put together an alterna-

tive coalition. Eventually it was decided to call a general election, which would take place in September. In August, I read that Phoolan had been selected by the Samajwadi Party to be their candidate again for Mirzapur. I wrote to wish her good luck.

Various factors favoured the BJP in the election campaign. Sonia Gandhi, the Italian-born widow of the assassinated Rajiv Gandhi, had been selected to lead the Congress, but this had caused dissention in the party. Moreover, the BJP-led government had recently fought a successful war against Pakistan-backed fighters who had invaded Indian-occupied Kashmir. The bookmakers made the BJP odds-on favourites to win the election. This did not bode well for Phoolan, whose opponent at Mirzapur was the BJP man who had taken the seat from her the year before. Moreover, the lower-caste vote was likely to be split. The Dalit-dominated BSP of Mayawati was fielding an ex-minister who had personally supervised the police operations against Phoolan's gang in the aftermath of the Behmai killings. He took every opportunity to denounce Phoolan's past. Nevertheless, there were reports that Phoolan was conducting a good campaign. Umed Singh, described as her 'ex-husband', was absent. Phoolan was depicted as being 'quieter, the quick anger replaced by the patience of a politician'.

As predicted, the BJP coalition won the election by a wide margin. The British media reported that Congress had been humiliated and that the BJP would be able to form a stable government with little fear of being ousted. I had an anxious few days as I waited to learn what had happened in Mirzapur. To my astonishment Phoolan had won by a landslide. She had polled over 84,000 votes more than the BJP runner-up. The BSP candidate polled less than half of Phoolan's tally. I tried to phone Chittaranjan Park but the line was constantly engaged. I dashed off a letter to congratulate Phoolan. I wrote that although I realised she would be very busy, I did hope it might still be possible for us to visit Chitrakut.

A couple of weeks later, I managed to get through on the phone. Phoolan was away, but I spoke to Sarfraaz. He said that Phoolan was expecting me and that she was keen to accompany me to Chitrakut. I told him that I had just booked a flight to Delhi and would be staying in India for a month.

*

I flew into Delhi on 6 November. At Chittaranjan Park, I found Phoolan's sister Munni, with Hargobind and their two children. Santosh, Phoolan's nephew, was there too, as well as his sister Usha. There was an air of excitement about the house as Usha, still probably a teenager, was about to become engaged. Conveniently for me, the English-speaking Sarfraaz was also in residence. Phoolan was in Mirzapur when I arrived but returned early next morning. To my surprise, since I had read that they were estranged, she was with Umed. She looked well and was very cheerful – particularly so, since it was the feast of Divali, the festival of lights. When Ram, the god-king, had returned to Ayodhya, he had been welcomed by a multitude of lamps. This welcome for the god was replicated every year by all Hindus. In North India, Holi and Divali were the two most important events in the Hindu calendar.

The apartments were cleaned from top to bottom. We went out and bought hundreds of little earthenware bowls, which were then filled with oil and a wick, and we bought hundreds of candles too. These lamps and candles were placed in front of the apartments, on every possible wall and railing. We decorated the house with coloured paper streamers. The children painted a cow that regularly came down the road to receive the customary first chapatti of the day with a pattern of green spots. A statue of Lakshmi – the goddess of wealth, whose day it was – was placed in front of Phoolan's racks of holy images. Lamps and sticks of incense were lit and prayers offered up. As soon as it was dark all the other lamps and candles were ignited. Phoolan put a red tilak on the foreheads of us men and popped huge sweets into our mouths.

Then it was time for fireworks. Massive quantities had been bought. Rockets, 'atomic-bombs' and huge 'jumping-jacks' were set off with no regard to safety. The children were allowed to light even the most dangerous. Phoolan set off a Catherine wheel inside the apartment and burnt a carpet. All the houses around us were participating. The night sky of Delhi was lit up; the noise was deafening. Jackie, the Great Dane, cowered in the basement. It made Guy Fawkes Night in Britain look very tame. Great palls of smoke drifted across the city, which lingered for days.

Sitting in London, I had carefully worked out an itinerary for my visit. This was thrown into disarray by Usha's impending engagement ceremonies, about which I had known nothing. The ceremony would be held in Jhansi in three days' time. Moreover, the son of her party leader, Mulayam Singh, was to be married in Etawah District, on the 22nd. Phoolan had been invited and wanted me to accompany her. From Etawah, Phoolan suggested, we could proceed to Chitrakut to look for a house.

We talked about her election victory in Mirzapur.

'It all came to a head very early on,' she said. 'The boss of the local illicit-brewing mafia tried to stop me lodging my nomination papers. He surrounded the government offices with armed men. But I was ready for him,' she smiled. 'This time I had plenty of manpower. I collected six hundred men with guns and we marched straight through. After that it was all very peaceful!'

'And what's happened to your court case?'

'It's been possible to delay matters by moving the case from one court to another. I don't think anything much will happen for some time. The lawyers are taking all my money, but at least I'm free.'

*

We left for Gwalior by train. As we were leaving, I suddenly realised that Usha was not with us. When I raised the alarm, I was looked at with amazement. Then everyone laughed. A bride-to-be was not part of an engagement ceremony.

At Gwalior local politicians greeted us and covered Phoolan in garlands. There was also an army of reporters. Phoolan made a little speech. Shiv Narayan had come and soon we were whisked off to his house. This was the very smart new bungalow that had been the subject of envy in the rest of the family. It was a modern architect-designed cubist building with attractive balconies and ironwork. It was finished in tasteful orange ochre. It could not have been more different from the village house of his childhood.

The gifts that the prospective bride's family would give the bridegroom's family were piled up inside. Usha's mother, Rukhmani, and her eldest brother, Mathura Prasad, joined us. Her grandmother, Moola, had come from the village. When everyone was assembled, a series of complex rituals followed to bless the gifts. Sarfraaz had stayed behind in Delhi to study, so I had been deprived of my translator. Not for the last time that trip, I really did not know what was happening. For some reason the men covered their heads with a cloth during the ceremony. I had to take a sweet in one hand and a coconut in the other while Phoolan put a tilak on my forehead. Later I accompanied Rukhmani back to the little police house where she was staying so that she could milk their cows. These had been painted with small red circles for Divali.

Next morning we were supposed to leave for Jhansi at 10 a.m. Of course, it never happened. It had been decided that the groom would be given a motorbike. At 11 a.m. we began to scour Gwalior for a suitable model. Motorcycle after motor-cycle was taken out of a showroom for the men to test by roaring round the block at speed. When a decision was finally made, Phoolan took an age to beat down the price. Hargobind was delegated to drive the motorcycle to Jhansi. As it had neither number plates nor insurance and there were no helmets, I declined an invitation to ride pillion.

The delays exacerbated family tensions. Rukhmani, the bride-to-be's mother, complained that none of her friends were there and stormed off. Moola went with her. We eventually left in three vehicles at 4.30 p.m. Jhansi was only sixty-five miles south but we had three punctures and only arrived at 7.30. We went to a community centre where 'breakfast' was laid out for us. We freshened up and then went to a house of the bridegroom's family. It was a large building with a lawn in front. They were a family of prosperous ginger merchants. Everywhere was festooned with fairy lights; large chandeliers hung from the ceilings. We were ushered into a room whose walls had been entirely covered with tapestries of real flowers – marigolds, roses and jasmine. I was introduced to the bride-groom's father and uncles. Then we sat down for the ceremony of giving presents. Our people unpacked box after box of dried fruit, nuts, sweets, cloth and saris. There were also two suits for the bridegroom and, of course, the motorbike. I was delegated to tick each item off once the bridegroom's party confirmed that it was as had been promised. Fortunately, there were no discrepancies. We then adjourned to the balcony for an excellent vegetarian meal.

Later, we moved to a large room that had been lined with drapes so as to resemble a marquee. Again, all was festooned with lights and chandeliers. The bridegroom-to-be, Bhagwan Das, sat in front of a large floral tableau. He wore a white silk shirt with a red tie and a white cloth covered his head. He had a handsome young face but looked very sombre. Umed sat beside him and discussed points of etiquette with the Hindu priest. There was much cracking of coconuts, arranging of holy plants and sprinkling of holy water. Of late Umed had become very keen on religious ceremony. The priest led Bhagwan Das through the affirmation of his engagement to the absent Usha, whom he had not yet met. The marriage had been organised entirely by Phoolan. She was very fond of Usha and I was confident that she would have arranged a good match.

As soon as the ceremony was over, Shiv Narayan and some other men rushed outside. There was a tremendous din as they fired their rifles and pistols into the air. We then sat out on the lawn for the main meal. As we had already eaten twice within the past two hours, I ate little. Others were less inhibited. I saw many take second and even third helpings. Again the meal was vegetarian but with many special dishes and sweets only served at such ceremonies. I talked to Bhagwan Das, who turned out not to be at all sombre. Now the official business was over, he was constantly smiling and laughing. I told him he was very lucky to be marrying Usha. I meant it, for she had always been one of my favourites. When a troop of drummers arrived I was dragged off to join the men in a shambolic dance.

We left for Gwalior at 10.30 p.m. – three hours and three meals after our arrival. We had more punctures on the return journey and did not get back until 3 a.m. Nevertheless, everyone was in an excellent mood. Phoolan was beaming. The day, she thought, had gone well.

Next morning we all went to visit Gwalior Jail. Phoolan wanted to meet her old friends and give them some presents. We were greeted by the same superintendent that I had met in 1992. He took my hand and squeezed it between his fat bejewelled fingers. He behaved as if we were old friends. We sat in his huge office for an hour while Phoolan questioned him about conditions in the jail. I gathered that some of the inmates had complained to her. Eventually, Phoolan was allowed into the jail, accompanied by warders carrying a multitude of boxes that contained snacks and sweets, clothes and perfume. She tried to take me with her but the superintendent refused permission. He claimed that he had instructions from his superiors that barred foreigners from entry. I stayed behind with the women and children until a happy Phoolan re-emerged. We then all went for lunch at the superintendent's house. I doubted that Phoolan had come to regard him with affection, but assumed that she thought it politic to be polite for the sake of her friends in his jail. I, similarly, was effusive with my thanks for his hospitality.

Afterwards we made a lightning tour of the houses of Phoolan's friends and political allies. We drank innumerable cups of tea and ate mountains of sweets. There was just time to visit the tomb of Tansen, the revered sixteenth-century singer and musician, before we caught the train back to Delhi.

The train was full. Phoolan was in a seat next to the inter-carriage door that for some reason was being propped open by a man. Politely, she asked him to move. He then directed a tirade of abuse at her, saying that he knew who she was and that she was now an MP but who was she of all people to tell him what to do. Hargobind moved to calm him down. He then grabbed Hargobind quite violently. I was surprised that the police bodyguard did nothing, but perhaps he did not want to be distracted. However, the diminutive Hargobind needed no assistance. He dragged the man into the corridor between the carriages and thrashed him. Travelling with Phoolan as she met her admirers and deferential officials, it was easy to forget that many in India disliked her intensely, and that they bitterly resented that she had ever been allowed to leave prison and enter parliament.

That day there had been a one-day international cricket match at Gwalior. India had beaten New Zealand. There had been a large, happy crowd at the railway station trying to get home. Phoolan had needed to assert her status as an MP to get tickets for us. On the train, I went off to the toilet and, on my return, was stopped by a very tall man who enquired what the recent fracas with Hargobind had been about. I sat down with him and explained. We then talked of the cricket match. He had been at the match. I gave my views on the pitch and tactics, with which he good-naturedly agreed. We discussed Phoolan and he was sympathetic. He suggested he might visit us at the house and I gave him the telephone number. I returned to my own seat.

'What did he want?' someone asked.

'Oh, he just wanted to know what the dispute was about. Then we talked about cricket. He's a nice chap and he might visit us. I wonder who he is.'

'You mean you don't know!' Everyone looked at me in amazement. It was as if I had just come from Mars. 'That's Ravi Shastri! He captained India! He once scored six sixes in an over!'

That evening everyone was still talking incessantly of the possibility that Ravi Shastri might favour us with a visit. I realised then what true fame was for most in India – not that of politicians, but that of film stars and cricketers.

*

There was a gap of a few days before we would set out from Delhi for the wedding of Mulayam Singh's son in Etawah, so I decided to make a quick visit to the northern hills. I went to Almora, but found it too cold and moved on to Haridwar and Rishikesh. At Rishikesh I had an unpleasant experience. A man in the room above me drank too much and tipped over his balcony, past my window, to his death on the concrete below. For some reason the police declined to move the body and it lay for the hours until I left in a large pool of blood that accumulated flies. I was glad to return to Delhi.

*

I gave Phoolan a shawl I had bought for her in Haridwar. She berated me for wasting my money.

'People give me lots of gifts,' she said, 'but I don't really need them. I give most of them away. All I need is two chapattis a day!'

It was true that she spent very little on show. She had a car, but she needed that for her political work. The house was frugally furnished. We ate the kind of food enjoyed by better-off peasants. Most unusually for a politician, she employed no servants and would join in doing the housework.

'What kind of present should I buy for the big wedding in Etawah?' I asked.

'Why bother?' she replied. 'Those people have more money than you!'

*

We took the early train for Kanpur. Umed, who seemed to be getting more religious by the day, set all four phones in the house to ring at 4 a.m. so that he could do various pujas before we left to catch the 6.20 train. Kanpur was one of my least favourite cities in India. It was crowded and the air was heavily polluted. There were piles of stinking rubbish everywhere. On the Mall there were some attractive art-deco buildings but they were horribly dilapidated. We checked into a small and not very clean hotel, where I shared a room with Umed. Phoolan had scheduled various political meetings and had booked herself into the City Club.

Next morning I was again woken at 4 a.m. by Umed as he performed some elaborate puja that required many bowls of water and much ringing of handbells. We then picked up Phoolan at 5.30. So far, we were on schedule for the wedding ceremony. Inevitably this could not last and we were soon on a round of politicians' houses to take tea and sweets. We finally left for Etawah at 9.30. It was a three-hour journey on potholed roads. A multitude of others were heading in the same direction. They were flying, like us, the red and green flag of the Samajwadi Party with its central motif of a bicycle. This bicycle fluttered from the bonnets of many large and expensive vehicles. As we neared Etawah it became clear that we were late. A flag-bearing stream was coming back towards us. The ceremony had been due to begin at 10 a.m. and, to our surprise, it had.

The wedding was held beyond Etawah in the tiny village that Mulayam Singh had come from. It was not a typical Uttar Pradesh village. Small as it was, it was full of fine new buildings. These included a hospital that looked as though it had been designed by a first-class architect. We had missed the ceremony but no one seemed bothered. Many cars were still arriving. The field that was being used was still packed. Thousands of women wore beautiful and expensive saris. Their menfolk were dressed, as was mandatory for most politicians in India, like peasants. Their clothes were in khadi, the home-spun and hand-woven cotton cloth championed by Mahatma Gandhi in response to factory-made British imports. It was a fabric that was cool in summer and warm in winter. It could look smart, but the politicians left it baggy and wrinkled in an attempt to look like the village labourers they pretended to be in sympathy with, and whose votes they coveted.

There were dozens of huge marquees, graded according to the status of the guests, which were serving vast amounts of food. I was told that in all there were sixty thousand guests. I seemed to be the only European there. Every few minutes someone would come over and ask me, 'Are you from the BBC?' Mulayam Singh wandered through the throng being affable to all. He stopped to talk to Phoolan and I was introduced. He was a stocky man of fifty, still strongly built like the champion wrestler he had been. He wore the simple white kurta that was his trademark. There was stubble on his chin. He seemed quite unremarkable. It was only the presence of numerous fawning acolytes that gave a hint of his power. Men and women like him were the new maharajas and maharanis of India.

We went to see the married couple. They were inside a small house to which access was only given to those of importance. Phoolan took me in. The bride and groom sat on simple plastic chairs. Akhilesh Yadav had the facial features of his father, Mulayam Singh, but was in a smart cream silk jacket. He greeted us warmly. Phoolan told me that he was to follow his father into politics. The bride, Dimple, was in a maroon and white sari with a tasselled matching shawl. Her hands were elaborately patterned with henna, her arms heavy with bangles. She wore an elaborate multiple-stringed gold necklace. A gold chain ran down the red ochred parting of a married woman to dangle a gold medallion over her forehead. Following tradition, she kept her eyes always downcast. I took a photograph as Phoolan put her hand on top of the bride's head to bless her.

*

We drove back to Kanpur to catch the train south-east to Chitrakut. Umed returned to Delhi. We were joined by some of Phoolan's associates, who would accompany her to Mirzapur after she left Chitrakut. She had arranged for a fellow caste member, Vishambhar Prasad Nishad, to come with us. He was a politician and knew Chitrakut well. Phoolan had bought food for us all, but I noticed that she herself did not eat. She looked tired. The train was delayed and we finally arrived at the unlit station at 1.30 a.m. As we stepped off the train I was startled when out of the darkness a brass band struck up. A large crowd surged forward shouting – 'Phoolan Devi *zindabad*' – 'Long live Phoolan Devi!' The noise was such that it awoke the entire train. Startled faces peered out of its windows.

Chitrakut station was actually at Karvi, about five miles from

Chitrakut itself. Fortunately, it had been decided to concentrate the area's administrative buildings in Karvi so as to minimise any impact on Chitrakut. We dropped off Phoolan and her bodyguards at the government resthouse and the rest of us checked into a scruffy hotel.

In the morning we went off to look at the religious sights. First of all, however, we had to visit the police station to check that it was safe to travel about. Dadua Patel, a notorious bandit, had been terrorising the area and kidnapping for ransom. (Dadua was also deeply involved in politics. At various times he had given assistance to different political parties. It was said that politicians needed his blessing to win seats in some thirty local districts.) Assured that Dadua was elsewhere, we set off for an ashram ten miles along the River Mandakini that was dedicated to Sati Anusuya, who was believed to have created the river through her meditation. It was a wonderful drive through a thick forest full of flowers, birds and monkeys. The ashram was on the bank of the river. It was a simple stone building with an open front and steps leading down to the water. The priests made us very welcome. Phoolan gave them a large wad of banknotes. She asked me whether I fancied living near there, which might be possible. It was such a beautiful place that I was tempted, but realistically it was too isolated and I turned it down.

We went on to Hanuman Dhara and climbed the three-hundred-plus steps to where the water gushed out of the rocks. In a Hindu epic it had sustained Hanuman the monkey god on his journey back from Lanka. There was a splendid panoramic view over the Chitrakut countryside.

In the afternoon Phoolan addressed a rally. She looked tired and had a cough. Nevertheless, she was still able to deliver a speech in her usual barnstorming manner and received rapturous applause. As I watched her speak a man came up to me and demanded to know who I was. When I asked him what it was to him, he produced his Intelligence Bureau identification card. He looked sceptical when I told him I was travelling with Phoolan and he took down my details. I heard nothing more but imagined my presence must have gone on file to join the many other baffled entries against my name.

After the rally Phoolan and her retinue left by road to travel the hundred and twenty miles east to Mirzapur. One of the great advantages of locating myself in Chitrakut was its proximity to Phoolan's constituency. In an emergency, she told me, she would be able to send me speedy assistance. Before she left she found a party worker, Ram, who would act as a guide and help me in my search for a property. I moved from Karvi into the same Chitrakut hotel overlooking the river that I had stayed in the year before.

*

Next morning, we started to look for properties. Ram turned out to be fairly useless. He tried to interest me in some vacant plots, although I had told him that I had no intention of building a new house. He brought along a friend who supposedly spoke English. In fact his English was minimal and, moreover, he turned up in the evening completely drunk. I got rid of him. Ram and I took a boat along the river to see if there were any possibilities just beyond the town. The boatman, Basant Lal, turned out to be much more helpful. I pointed to various properties and he seemed to know who the owners were and whether they might be for sale.

He and Ram took me to see the local Raja, who had asked to meet me. (Legally, of course, he was not a raja, for Indira Gandhi had abolished all titles in 1971. Nevertheless, many ex-rajas, maharajas, nawabs, etc., continued to have large properties, and continued to be referred to by their former titles.) Wandering around the lanes on the north bank of the

Mandakini I had noticed a large concrete wall. I was surprised to find that behind it was an attractive crenelated palace. Massive entrance doors were flanked by polished brass cannon. Inside, I found a classic storybook raja with a round face bearing a large white cavalry moustache. He was seated on a bolstered throne.

We discussed my search for a property. It turned out that he wanted to sell me a useless little plot against the concrete outer wall. After I had politely turned it down, we went back into his palace to take tea. He relaxed back onto his throne.

'So,' he said, 'what are current attitudes in Britain regarding us in India?'

Slightly taken aback, I launched into an assessment of British reactions to the fiftieth anniversary of Indian independence.

'No! No! – I meant, what about our privy purses? The British guaranteed an income to us rajas and our descendants. Then they left without making any proper arrangements. Mrs Gandhi took the money away. What are the British going to do about their obligations?'

'Well,' I strove to be diplomatic, 'I don't think it's on the agenda at the moment.'

'Surely your House of Lords will do something.'

'Well,' I said, 'I wouldn't be too optimistic. There are plans afoot for the House of Lords itself to be abolished.'

I left him looking upset and bemoaning his lot.

(Some time later, I was amused to come across a reference to the origin of the Raja's family. The British had given a Lachhman Singh the title and rights over five villages in 1807. These had been offered as an inducement for him to surrender, for he had been a notorious dacoit.)

It was Basant Lal who finally found me something more interesting. Not far from the Raja's palace was an abandoned and dilapidated old fortified house. The property was about sixty feet square, enclosed by a twenty-foot-high stone wall. A balcony with elaborate arches surmounted an imposing gateway. This led into a courtyard. A large arched room lay at one end, with a flat roof. Stone staircases ascended to this roof. At each end of this were side rooms, again with decorated arches. The building was probably two centuries old and had obviously not been lived in for many years. The courtyard was full of rampant bushes; creepers covered the walls; there were cracks in the masonry; great chunks of plaster had fallen off. Nevertheless, the stonework was so thick that the overall impression was one of great underlying strength.

'The owner is a local priest,' Basant Lal told me. 'Ah, here he comes.'

Madan Tewari was probably in his thirties, tall, slim and moustached, and with a pleasant manner. He was dressed entirely in white – a long white shirt over white trousers, and a long white scarf around his neck. He told me that his family had owned the house for centuries. Decades ago, they had decided to move nearer to the river, so as to be close to the temple of which they were the hereditary priests.

'The place has been empty since then,' he said, 'sometimes we used it for our cows. We don't even use it for that now, so we would be prepared to sell.'

'How much do you want?' I asked.

'Three lakhs.'

Three lakhs was about £4,500. In the last few years my financial situation had improved, and I thought I might be able to raise that. I toyed with the idea of bargaining, but decided against it. I thought it better to leave that to Phoolan. I would do a rough survey of the house and talk over the possibility of restoring it with her. If she thought it feasible, I would mull matters over before making a decision. It was a big step. There seemed to be no nearby source of water other than the river, which was several hundred yards away, and that might have been why Tewari's family had moved. Electricity would be another problem. I did not want to be throwing my money into a bottomless pit. If I decided to go ahead I could return with Phoolan next year. It would all depend on her opinion, for I would need her help in getting permissions for renovation. Nothing would be possible without her active support.

I gave some money to Ram and Basant Lal to reward them for their efforts.

'I'll be back,' I told them confidently.

I was already becoming more and more convinced that Chitrakut was the place for me. Moreover, I might have found the perfect house.

*

I left that evening by train to Agra and then by bus to the deserted Mughal capital of Fatehpur Sikri. While I was there, a fellow tourist told me that Phoolan had been robbed while walking in the street in Delhi. I thought it unlikely. From Fatehpur Sikri I went to the bird sanctuary at Bharatpur and then to the fort and palaces at Deeg. I returned to Delhi on 3 December.

*

Phoolan was back at Chittaranjan Park. Her sister Ramkali had arrived together with her delightful little Nandani. It was two years since I had seen them in the village. The hard life had taken its toll and Ramkali looked somewhat older, but she was still very attractive.

'Is it true that you were robbed?' I asked Phoolan.

'Well,' she gave a broad smile, 'not really. I was in a friend's car going to collect my medicines in Chittaranjan Park market. Some drunken students were blocking the road and our driver hooted at them. They then dragged him out of the car and beat him up. I reported it at the police station. I told the police that I had lost some money just to make them sit up and take notice.'

'So what happened?'

'Nothing. No one was arrested. But if I see those students again they'll be sorry!'

I told Phoolan about my time in Chitrakut and enthusiastically described the property I had found.

'The owner wants three lakhs.'

'It's too much,' she said. 'It should be one or two lakhs at the outside. No Indian would even consider buying such a place! Leave it to me. I'll make enquiries.'

'And I'll think things over,' I said. 'I really like this property. If it can be obtained for a reasonable price, I might buy it. However, it will cost a lot to put it in order and I need to think about what I can afford. I'll write to you from London.'

Next day we relaxed at Chittaranjan Park. Phoolan and Umed were leaving in the late evening for Lucknow and Mirzapur. I was completely unaware of this until the last minute. It was another example of how, probably because of my limited Hindi, I was constantly surprised by events. We talked again of Chitrakut. Phoolan was very keen on the idea of my going there.

'Come to Goa with us for New Year,' she urged. 'I'll pay for the hotel.'

She seemed very disappointed when I told her that it was impossible as I had used up all my leave entitlement.

'Ah, well,' she sighed, 'we'll meet again next year. Make sure you come early.'

*

In January 2000, I wrote to Phoolan to wish her a happy New Year. I described the millennium celebrations and then went on:

I have discussed the Chitrakut house with my family and friends, and decided to go ahead with the purchase. As you know, it was offered for three lakhs. I could manage that much, but it is so dilapidated that I hope it can be bought cheaper. About two lakhs might be a fair price, as it will cost a lot of money to make habitable. I leave it completely to your discretion to make the best deal for me, and will send the money as soon as you ask.

I attached a list of queries relating to the water, sewage, electricity and the boundaries of the property.

I was busy trying to find a publisher for my now finished book, *The Great Hedge of India*. This monopolised most of my spare time. I drew a blank with agents and the first dozen publishers that I wrote to. No one even wanted to read the manuscript. Then my luck changed. A couple of publishers showed interest and in April I signed a contract with Constable. I was now free to devote more of my energies to the Chitrakut project. I was already fantasising about writing a book about Chitrakut.

I was not the only person fantasising about Chitrakut. Lalu Prasad Yadav, the flamboyant former Chief Minister of Bihar (and now running the state by proxy through his wife), had been accused of perpetrating a huge fraud. Emerging from a temporary spell in jail, where he claimed to have spent his time studying religious texts, he announced that he wanted to retire from politics to 'a life of peace in Chitrakut'. Fortunately, it seemed unlikely.

I received an email from Sarfraaz, on Phoolan's behalf, inviting me to Usha's wedding. It was, however, totally impossible for me to be away from the library. After many efforts, I finally managed to get through on the phone to Chittaranjan Park. Phoolan was away but I did manage to speak to Usha herself and wish her luck.

Communications with India had recently been transformed. In the early years of my friendship with Phoolan, even after she had been released from jail, letters had been the only way to contact her. I would have to wait at least a month for a reply. Indian telephones had been notoriously unreliable. Now, there was no problem with the phones, only that Phoolan's was often busy. Email was another major advance, which Sarfraaz was keen to use. India no longer seemed so distant and inaccessible. I received regular reports from Phoolan about Chitrakut negotiations. She suggested that I should try to visit India that June or July.

Phoolan was still living in Chittaranjan Park. She should have moved into one of the official residences for MPs in central New Delhi. As usual, however, previous occupants, who had probably lost their seats in parliament, were proving difficult to evict from their free accommodation. I also read that Phoolan was not endearing herself to the smarter residents of Chittaranjan Park. They had protested about the presence of slum-dwellers in their neighbourhood and had urged the authorities to demolish their shacks. This had a certain irony, as many of these posher residents had themselves been refugees from Bangladesh before being rehoused. Phoolan had championed the slum-dwellers. She had threatened to lead a protest if the municipal authorities tried to take action. She seemed to have won that argument.

In May, there were reports from Chitrakut of fake 'encounters'. In one case, the police had picked up a young and harmless man. They had intended to kill him and then pretend that he was a bandit in order to boost their anti-banditry statistics. Fortunately, his parents had been able to enlist the help of a minister. In a judicial raid on the police station, their son had been found, tortured and injured, but alive.

Not all 'encounters' in Uttar Pradesh were fake. Lala Ram, the bandit leader who had been instrumental in Phoolan's imprisonment and multiple rape at Behmai, was betrayed to the police. He had also been the prime mover of the 'widows' marches' from Behmai that had been used to try to undermine Phoolan's position. Although he was wanted for a multitude of murders and kidnappings, his popularity among his Thakur upper caste had enabled him to avoid capture for thirty years. He was found visiting his mistress near to Kanpur, then shot.

Phoolan was still supposed to be on trial for the murders in Behmai but all was quiet on that front. Another, rather bizarre, case against her had recently been reactivated. It was alleged that she had attacked a fellow prisoner at Gwalior Jail in 1986. She was accused of 'throwing slippers' at him. While Indian slippers were usually a good deal more solid than British ones, it seemed an extraordinarily trivial complaint. Nevertheless, a magistrate in Gwalior had ordered her to appear in court. I doubted that Phoolan would be worried.

*

I flew into Delhi early on 17 July. This was my first visit to India during the monsoon. Water lay deep everywhere and it was unpleasantly humid. The two flats at Chittaranjan Park were packed. Phoolan's sister Munni and family were in residence, as were Phoolan's husband, Umed, and the helpful Muslim student Sarfraaz. There were also at least a dozen distant relatives and hangers-on. It was a perennial problem for those in the public eye. Relatives they never even knew they had (and in India, where family ties are so important, this meant a very tenuous connection indeed) would descend on them for free board and lodging and to seek help in finding employment. Poor Munni was hard pressed to both look after her children and feed everyone.

Phoolan arrived late evening. She was furious to find her house so full.

'You are just spongers!' she told them, adding a few crude expletives. 'Get out!'

In spite of the late hour, a few did leave. The rest mumbled some apology and eventually went to sleep on one of the down-stairs floors. Jackie, the Great Dane, was crammed into a corner. Upstairs, one of the women entreated Phoolan to lie down and have her legs pressed. In India this massaging of the calf muscles was done not only to relax the legs but as a sign of respect. Phoolan acquiesced and she soon cheered up.

'I've just been to Kerala,' she told me. 'It was wonderful. So green. It was like a foreign country.'

'Will you be free some time to come to Chitrakut?'

'I have to go to Mirzapur. Parliament reconvenes on the 24th and I will have to be there for a couple of days. With any luck we can go to Chitrakut a few days after that. Don't worry, we'll get there eventually.'

*

I decided that there was no point in waiting around in Delhi. I went to Rajasthan for a few days to visit Pushkar and Ajmer. I knew that Phoolan was a regular visitor to the tomb of the Sufi saint Khwaja Muin-ud-din Chisti. I prayed at the shrine and brought her back a rose.

*

At Chittaranjan Park, Phoolan had just returned from Mirzapur. She looked extremely tired. Sarfraaz told me that there had been talk of Phoolan going to visit Britain that July. She had been invited by a group of her supporters in Birmingham.

'When are you off to the UK?' I asked.

'I've cancelled it.'

'But, why?'

'My stomach is still giving me problems.'

'Are you really sure you are up to travelling to Chitrakut?'

'Yes, yes,' she said and gave me a smile. 'We're definitely going. I'm looking forward to it.'

Later, Sarfraaz told me that she had not been keen to visit Britain with me not there. I felt rather selfish about prioritising my own trip to India. However, there was nothing I could do about it.

*

We left for Chitrakut on 26 July. There were just four of us – Phoolan, me, a bodyguard and a retired railway engine driver who often helped Phoolan. Umed had opted instead to go on a pilgrimage to a religious site in the Himalayas. We four took the afternoon train. It stopped at Gwalior, where Phoolan's brother, Shiv Narayan, came briefly on board to greet us and bring food.

Phoolan lay down on her berth and had the curtains to the corridor closed. I was keen to look out at the passing countryside, so sat in one of the seats on the opposite side of the corridor. Her bodyguard sat opposite me and we chatted. When he went off to the toilet, an inquisitive passenger took the vacant seat and started to interrogate me quite aggressively.

'Who are you?' he asked. 'Who is that woman you're with?'

'A friend.'

'Is she your wife?'

'No, no.'

'Then who is she?'

'Actually,' I said, fed up with his nosy questioning, 'it's Phoolan Devi.'

'Don't tell me that! Really, who is she?'

'I've told you – Phoolan Devi. Don't you believe me?'

'How could it be Phoolan Devi?' he said angrily. 'If that was Phoolan Devi she would be surrounded by men with guns.'

'I'm not going to argue,' I said. 'I've told you. I'm travelling with Phoolan Devi.'

At that moment the plainclothes bodyguard returned and gestured that he would like his seat back.

'For some reason,' the querulous passenger said, 'this European here insists on telling me that the woman with you is Phoolan Devi. Why is he saying that?'

'Because she is,' the bodyguard replied. He drew back his shirt to reveal his pistol. 'Now, get lost!'

The man stared at him in horror. For several seconds he stood transfixed. Then, without uttering a word, he fled to another carriage.

The incident had its amusing side, but it made me think about Phoolan's security. Since I had first met her, this had gradually been scaled back. Phoolan herself acquiesced in this because she wanted to lead what she called a 'normal life'. The fact was, however, that she was leading a far from normal life. In India almost all politicians had heavy security. A relatively insignificant MLA would often travel with half a dozen guards armed with sub-machine guns. Some of this, no doubt, was merely for prestige. However, from time to time the newspapers would carry a story of some politician being assassinated. It was good that Phoolan was not paranoid but I was worried that she was becoming too casual.

Our train arrived in Chitrakut at 5 a.m. We were met by Vishambhar Prasad Nishad, the local politician whom we had met the year before. He had booked some rooms for us in a dharmashala, a pilgrims' resthouse. We rested for a couple of hours then went off to a nearby temple to offer up prayers before returning to the dharmashala. Various people whom Phoolan and Vishambhar had summoned began to stream into Phoolan's bedroom. There were about fifteen local politicians, lawyers and land-registry officials crammed with us into the small room. Madan Tewari arrived. He beamed as he showed

Phoolan a certificate of solvency. This confirmed that there were no mortgages or other claims on the land. Phoolan took me on one side.

'Tewari told you that he wanted three lakhs, didn't he?' she whispered.

'Yes, but I did not agree a price. I told him we'd think about it.'

'Good. Well, I think that we are now ready to bargain.'

As she spoke, more people arrived. Three were lawyers and one of these was aggressively waving a piece of paper. There were heated exchanges in Hindi that I could not follow. Phoolan looked perturbed.

As the arguments went on, the overcrowded room became insufferably hot. Everyone was perspiring. Vishambhar, who had the classic wrestler-like build of a politician from Uttar Pradesh, was looking uncomfortable. Eventually, he took off his long shirt. Beneath it he was wearing a vest. Crossed over this were two straps each slotted with bullets. In a holster on each there was a pistol.

'Goodness!' I exclaimed. 'What are those for?'

'Best to be safe,' he replied with a grin. 'You never know what will happen in a place like Chitrakut.'

As I mulled over this somewhat disquieting remark, the noisy exchanges continued. Tewari looked very upset. Finally, the shouting subsided and everyone looked glum.

'What's happening?' I anxiously asked Vishambhar.

'There are problems, big problems,' he told me. 'Tewari's ownership is being contested by three separate people. Two are relatives. One of these has already taken the matter to court. The other objection is from the head priest of the nearby temple. He is claiming that half the land that the house was constructed on originally belonged to the temple and that it was built on illegally.'

'My God! Where does that leave us?'

'It looks very bad. I doubt that we can go ahead.'

I looked at Phoolan.

'This is India!' she said sadly.

The meeting broke up. Basant Lal, the boatman who had found the original house, offered to show me another property. We went off to look at a small building encircling a courtyard. It had some nice decorative features, and although it had obviously not been inhabited for many years, it was not too dilapidated. It belonged to the Raja.

'How much does he want?' I asked.

'I'll go and ask,' Basant Lal replied and rushed off.

I took a number of photographs and started to measure things up. Gradually, I was overcoming my earlier disappointment and becoming enthusiastic again. Basant Lal soon returned. He looked glum.

'I was wrongly informed,' he said. 'It's not for sale!'

I made my way back to the dharmashala feeling very low. My dreams, it seemed, were not going to be realised. Maybe the relatives could be bought off but the temple objection was much more serious. Even if the matter went to court and they lost, I would then be at daggers drawn with a powerful local temple. This, in India, would be disastrous.

When I arrived, I was astonished to find Phoolan all smiles. She was with Madan Tewari and he was smiling too. Vishambhar explained what had happened.

Phoolan had persuaded Mr Tewari to buy out the other claimants. She had then beaten down his asking price of three lakhs to one-and-a-half lakhs. This was to include not only the house but also the piece of land in front, which was roughly the same area as the house. The tax on the transfer together with other fees would come to another half lakh. This made two lakhs (£3,000) in total. It was a stupendous bargain.

'Thank you so much,' I said to Phoolan. 'I'm extremely happy.'

'So am I!'

Vishambhar replaced his shirt and, together with Tewari and all the local officials and politicians, posed with Phoolan and me for group photographs.

Although the deal had been made there would, of course, be a good deal of paperwork to be done before the transfer was official. Being India, where bureaucratic delays on property transfers were legendary, this was liable to take a very long time. There was no point in my hanging around so I decided to return to Delhi with Phoolan. We would catch the evening train. Before we left, Phoolan introduced me to the chairman of the panchayat, the village council, of the area in which the house lay. He promised to help me in every possible way. She also telephoned the Raja, who assured her that he would give me any assistance I needed. Later, she introduced me to a local woman politician who was exceptionally friendly. She was very amusing and was soon making plans to marry me off to her widowed sister.

At dusk, Basant Lal took us for a trip down the river. He had carpeted his boat with new decorative mats. On the framework of the awning above the boat he had hung a multitude of gold and silver tassels. It was the time of day that the temple priests went down to the river's edge with lamps on trays to perform *aarti*. They slowly described circles with the illuminated trays as they sang hymns to their favourite deities. The view from the centre of the river was magical.

It was totally dark as we rushed to catch the train. The monkeys that resided in the station rafters had closed their eyes. The train was slightly late. This gave me enough time to profusely thank Vishambhar, and the multitude of politicians and officials who had been so helpful, before we boarded for Delhi.

*

I was only in Delhi for a couple of days. Phoolan was extremely busy. Our short trip to Chitrakut had put her behind schedule. Once we returned to Chittaranjan Park she was continually closeted with people needing her assistance. Among others, there was a Canadian of Indian origin who wanted help to set up a satellite TV channel that was not dominated by the upper castes. A large delegation came from an organisation in northern Uttar Pradesh, an area that was about to break away to become the new state of Uttaranchal (now Uttarkhand). They wanted Phoolan's assistance in framing a reservation policy for the lower castes. Every day, there were dozens of individual supplicants with personal problems trying to get help from Phoolan. She was amazingly patient but it was a drain on her health. By evening, she usually looked exhausted. Moreover, she was just about to go on another extensive tour of North India, where there would be, no doubt, many meetings and many speeches to deliver. While she would be away from Delhi I took the opportunity to travel myself.

*

I left for Gujarat on 29 July. I took the train to Ahmedabad, visited the palaces of Bhavnagar and Junagadh, saw the hundreds of Jain temples at Palitana and swam from the beaches of the former Portuguese enclave of Diu, before I returned to Delhi on 10 August.

*

Delhi was being battered by heavy rain. There were murky pools of unknown depth on the roads. My auto-rickshaw went down one of these and the engine stopped. I waded to safety, found another lift with difficulty and eventually arrived at Chittaranjan Park still soaked. Usha greeted me and laughed.

She looked as though marriage suited her. I gave her the crystal wedding presents I had brought for her from London. Her new husband was busy running the family's ginger business in Jhansi. As the women of the family never travelled without a man, Santosh had accompanied her. It was good to meet him again and reminisce about our past adventures.

Phoolan arrived back from parliament later in the day. She looked terribly tired and told me that her stomach was hurting. Nevertheless, she gave an interview for Star TV on the Veerappan affair, which was dominating the news.

Veerappan, a Tamil from the south, was now the most famous active bandit in India. He specialised in poaching elephants for their ivory and in the illicit logging of sandalwood. He ran a vendetta against Forestry Department officials, who he alleged had oppressed the forest dwellers. He and his gang had killed a great many. Several police officers had also been killed. Special task forces from three states had been pursuing him for ten years without success. Veerappan also specialised in kidnapping, either for ransom or to make other demands. At the end of July, in Tamil Nadu, he had kidnapped the most popular cinema actor in Karnataka, Rajkumar. A debate was raging as to whether or not the authorities should accede to Veerappan's demands. Many thought he should be granted a pardon, in order to secure Rajkumar's release. There had been suggestions that Veerappan wanted to enter politics. Inevitably, parallels were being drawn between Veerappan and Phoolan. These made Phoolan livid.

'Veerappan is just a criminal!' she told me. 'He has killed hundreds of innocent people. I never killed anyone that was innocent and yet I was imprisoned for eleven years! Why should he be pardoned just to obtain the release of a film star?'

Before I left for London, there was a fresh crisis over the Chitrakut house. Phoolan received a message that another four people had come forward to claim a share of the property. She thought they could be bought off quite cheaply. Once again she spread her hands and said, 'This is India.' Despite Phoolan's relaxed response I found this new development depressing. How many more objections would there be? Was this a fore-taste of problems to come? With these questions in my mind I was beginning to wonder, once again, if I should pull out of this quixotic adventure.

It turned out that the four objectors required, in total, only 5,000 rupees – that was £75. We agreed to that. Next day we heard from Chitrakut that the matter had been settled and that there were unlikely to be any more claimants. All seemed set fair. I left for Britain full of optimism.

*

Shortly after I returned to London in August, I sent Phoolan the two lakhs for the Chitrakut house. Soon afterwards I was star-tled to learn that the bandit Dadua Patel had once again been terrorising the countryside around Chitrakut. He had been seeking revenge on a villager for unspecified reasons. When Dadua found the man, who was together with his two grown sons, the three of them were beaten with bamboo staves and then shot. Once again, I began to wonder if Chitrakut would be too dangerous for me.*

Phoolan's stomach problems incapacitated her in the closing months of 2000. Eventually she had an operation,

---

* Dadua Patel continued to operate in the Chitrakut area for seven more years. In Chitrakut, in July 2007 a Special Task Force of the Uttar Pradesh police gunned down four members of his gang. This led them next day to Dadua, who was a few miles away, hidden in the rocks. Using hand-grenades, the police killed Dadua and five of his gang. The *Times of India* report added that the Uttar Pradesh government had spent huge sums in operations against Dadua since 1982, when he had gunned down eight people belonging to the upper castes, and that there were more than a hundred and eighty-five criminal cases pending against him.

which seemed to improve her health. When I telephoned Delhi, I might occasionally manage to speak to her, but often she was away in Mirzapur or on tour. She urged me to return to India as soon as I could, since the Chitrakut property transfer was ready to be finalised. I booked my annual leave for March.

In January my book *The Great Hedge of India* was published. It was more successful than I had imagined possible. I was extremely busy with a series of interviews and talks. In addition it was a busy time at the university library, where we were planning to move some collections into a new controlled-environment facility. Despite all this activity, I was anxious to build on the success of my book and was looking at possible themes for a new one.

One idea that I was investigating was to walk across India. I had been surprised to discover that the mighty River Krishna, which flowed into the eastern ocean, has its source near Mumbai at Mahabaleshwar, which was only forty miles from the western ocean. I thought that maybe I could write of my adventures crossing India on a walk down that river. I would need to make a preliminary reconnaissance. I telephoned Delhi and discussed my itinerary with Phoolan. She expected to be busy in early March, but assured me she would be free to travel with me to Chitrakut later in the month.

'Everything is ready to be signed,' she said. 'I'm looking forward to a little holiday.'

I therefore arranged to fly into Mumbai, visit Mahabaleshwar, and then go on to Delhi.

*

I flew into Mumbai on 4 March 2001. I telephoned Phoolan to check that my itinerary still suited her. She sounded cheerful and very keen to make another trip to Chitrakut. The following day, I travelled to the old British hill-station of Mahabaleshwar.

I went to the Panchganga temple, which was 4,500 feet above sea level. Inside, there was a stone sculpture of a cow's head. From its mouth flowed water. This was believed to be the source of five rivers, including the Krishna. Next day, I climbed down into the Krishna valley. A trek down the river seemed possible. I would need to give it more thought, and see how I could integrate such a time-consuming project with my library job, before I approached a publisher. From Mahabaleshwar I went to look at Shivaji's spectacular fort at Pratapgad, and then went on to visit the sea fort at Janjira. From Janjira I back-tracked to Mumbai to catch the train to Delhi.

*

I arrived in Delhi on 14 March. Phoolan had at last managed to move into her official MP's residence. As before it was in Ashok Road, but it was now at No. 44. The large colonial bungalow was almost identical to the residence she had been allocated in 1997, but it was in much better condition. It also had a large garden with trees and flowers. Jackie, the Great Dane, had space to roam. Phoolan was away in the eastern state of Assam but was expected back the next day. The house was full. There was Phoolan's husband, Umed, and her nephew Santosh. Her sister Munni and husband, Hargobind, together with their two children were also in residence. Mathura Prasad was visiting from Gwalior and had brought along his wife and two children too. Then there was 'Panditji', a Brahmin adviser to Phoolan, and her Keralite secretary, F. M. Das. There was also, of course, a police bodyguard. Everyone was in the living room watching the cricket on television. India were making a remarkable recovery from following on against Australia and it looked likely they might force an unlikely draw. This had put everyone in a festive mood.

The house was large, but since the rooms were huge there

were relatively few of them. There were not enough beds for everyone and many slept on the floor. I managed to find a camp bed and slept well in the quiet of a hallway.

Phoolan did arrive back the next evening. She made an effort to greet me with enthusiasm. She looked dreadfully tired, however, and was not her usual cheerful self. Almost immediately she went to bed.

Next morning Phoolan seemed to have recovered her spirits. She relaxed at home and watched the cricket on television. In her village she had never had access to radio or television. Nor, of course, had she for the eleven years that she had been in jail. With these now available she had discovered a new world. For someone who was illiterate, as she was, they made it considerably easier to understand events. Television had made the inability to read newspapers much less of a disadvantage. Over the years I had known her, she had gradually been transformed into a cricket fan. She spoke knowledgeably about the abilities of V. V. S. Laxman and Harbhajan Singh. The match, against all expectations, was won by India. At Phoolan's request, I went out with Santosh to buy celebratory sweets for all.

Later in the day, there was bad news for me. Vishambhar Prasad, the politician who had accompanied Phoolan and me to Chitrakut, came to see us. There had been more disputes within Madan Tewari's family over the transfer of the property. Until these were resolved there would be no point in our going to Chitrakut. Phoolan decided, therefore, to go to her constituency in Mirzapur for a few days. When she returned we would consider what to do. I was very dispirited by this latest setback. Perhaps foolishly, I had been confident that on this visit all was going to go smoothly.

'Can I come to Mirzapur with you?' I asked.

'No,' she said. 'I've explained to you before. It's too dangerous.'

'But I went in 1992 and it was fine.'

'Yes, but that was before people knew you were my friend. I am worried enough about my own security there. I don't want you killed too!'

I was kept busy while Phoolan was away. The UK edition of *The Great Hedge of India* was being sold in India and it had received good reviews. A paperback edition, published in India, was to be released in the near future. I gave a number of interviews to journalists. Some insisted on interviewing me at 'home'. When they came, they were amazed to find that I was staying with Phoolan Devi. I carefully parried their questions. Usually, I did not let them know that the Santosh who had helped me was Phoolan's nephew, or that the 'Didi' in my book was actually Phoolan. I had chosen the name deliberately as it translated as 'elder sister' and was in common use as an honorific. I did not want my story of the hedge to be swamped by the connection with Phoolan. Nevertheless, it was impossible to entirely hide my association with her, and the *Indian Express* played up her role as my 'secret helper'.

While Phoolan was away, Mirzapur was in the news. The police there had been in action against Naxalites, a name given to Maoist guerrillas who fought for the rights of the landless poor and tribal people. They were reported to have won a major gun-battle against the rebels. When Phoolan returned she told me that the media reports of a police victory were all false.

'The people that the police killed had done nothing wrong,' she told me, full of anger. 'The police pretended that sixteen of the poor were Naxalites, then shot them. They were innocent scapegoats, sacrificed to give the impression that the police were winning. I've done what I can for their families.'

There was some friction between Umed and Phoolan. In the past they had, I remembered, had differences that had caused them to part. I wondered if we were moving towards another crisis. Sometimes, when I got up in the middle of the night, I would find Phoolan dozing on the living-room floor.

Meanwhile, in Delhi there was a political crisis. An investigative website, Tehelka.com, had conducted a sting operation that seemed to show corruption in defence procurement. With secret cameras the journalists, posing as representatives of an arms company, had filmed political associates of the Minister of Defence accepting huge bribes inside the minister's house. The minister had resigned. The film was constantly replayed on television while in parliament the government was harried by the opposing parties. These, of course, included Phoolan's own Samajwadi Party. As the scandal developed, there was talk of a vote of confidence. Phoolan was needed in parliament.

'I'm sorry,' she told me, 'but it's quite impossible for me to come to Chitrakut at the moment. First, there is this Tehelka business. Secondly, the party want me to campaign at two by-elections in Uttar Pradesh.'

'Later in the month?'

'No, I'm afraid not. I've made some phone calls and it seems there are two factions in the Tewari family. I need to sit down with them and thrash it out. It could easily take five or six days!'

'Perhaps I should forget about that particular house and find somewhere else,' I said, deeply disappointed.

'No! No! It's only that it's not possible this month. Don't worry. Once parliament goes into recess, I'll go down there myself and, with Durga's help, sort it out.' She gave me a broad smile. 'You can rely on me.'

I decided that there was no point in my remaining in Delhi for the last week of my vacation. There was nothing I could achieve and the tension between Phoolan and Umed was souring the atmosphere. My plane would be departing from Mumbai. I thought that I might as well take the opportunity to travel to Mumbai by way of some places of interest in Rajasthan. Accordingly, I said goodbye to Phoolan and left Delhi the next morning. It was a decision I would come to regret.

8
The End of a Vendetta

'Such a person can be a role model
for the young generation.'

AFTER my return to London in April 2001, I was busy giving talks on *The Great Hedge of India* and looking at possibilities for a new book. I had decided to defer the project to walk the length of the River Krishna until after I had retired. When I had discussed what advance I was likely to obtain for such a book, I had realised that it would be insufficient for any prospect of early retirement. After another couple of false starts, I finally hit upon the idea of writing a book on the history of tea. As a young man I had been a tea planter in Africa, so it seemed feasible. I worked hard on a proposal and obtained a contract with a small advance.

While all this was going on I kept in touch with Phoolan. This was much easier than before. Not only had the phone link to her house improved but now she even had a mobile phone. We discussed the Chitrakut property. The family disputes over ownership were still rumbling on, but she was confident they could be resolved. I spoke to her in mid-July. She told me that she was intending to go to Chitrakut during August to finalise matters. Her health seemed to have taken a turn for the better. She sounded cheerful.

*

On 25 July, just a week after I had last spoken to her, Phoolan was assassinated.

I was at my workbench in the library when a friend from the British Library phoned to give me the news. It was difficult to believe. Soon, however, other friends had contacted me. I accessed the BBC website and saw that it was true.

In the early years of our friendship I had often thought that Phoolan might be killed. I remembered our first meeting, when the house had been surrounded by police with guns. Of how an officer had taken me up onto the roof to show me the excellent site he had chosen for his machine guns. In the years that followed, Phoolan's security had been progressively reduced. When we had gone to Chitrakut, only one bodyguard had accompanied us. In some ways Phoolan encouraged this. She wanted to lead as normal a life as possible. Nevertheless, she was always conscious that her enemies might seek revenge. She had often told me that she might be killed. In later years, unlike when she had written to me from prison, she did not really fear death. Perhaps this was because she had finally fulfilled some of her objectives. Phoolan had adopted the fatalism that was deep in the psyche of many Hindus. If it was destined to happen, it would happen.

I had no such solace. I felt sick. I felt as if I was about to fall and had to sit down. Then my immediate superior came to give me her condolences, took a look at me and sent me home. There, I lay down on my bed and mourned.

*

From the reports in the media, it appeared that Phoolan had returned at lunchtime from parliament to her house in Ashok Road. In front of the gates she had got down from her vehicle and walked towards the entrance. Three masked men then opened fire with handguns. Phoolan was shot in the body and the head. Her police bodyguard was hit twice, but managed to return fire before the assassins fled in a nearby car. The still conscious Phoolan lay on the ground unable to speak. As people hurried to her side, she was able to raise her hand. She was quickly transported to a neighbourhood hospital. Nothing could be done. She was dead.

Politicians rushed to the hospital. The Prime Minister made a short statement to parliament. After a tribute of a minute's silence, both houses adjourned for two days. A massive police manhunt was put in motion and all exits from Delhi were temporally closed. The get-away car was soon found. Inside were two revolvers, two pistols, ammunition and a brown 'monkey cap', a Balaclava-type helmet that covered all except the eyes. It appeared that the assailants had switched from their car to an auto-rickshaw and then managed to escape.

I knew that Hindus tried to cremate their dead within twenty-four hours of death, which would make it impossible for me to attend the funeral. I would have flown out to India if it had seemed there might be a delay, but events moved swiftly. In Delhi leading politicians, including the Prime Minister and the Leader of the Opposition, went to pay their respects to Phoolan, who lay in state at Ashok Road.

The day after the assassination, Phoolan's body was taken to Mirzapur. As there was no airport there, and time was of the essence, it was first flown to nearby Varanasi and then taken on by road. Over the entire state of Uttar Pradesh, shops and businesses closed from dawn to dusk. There, and as far away as Mumbai and Kolkata, effigies of the Prime Minister and Home Minister of India and of the Chief Minister of Uttar Pradesh were burnt. In Delhi, the Chief Minister of Uttar Pradesh's house was situated very close to that of Phoolan. At the time of the shooting his guards had failed to come to her assistance or to try to apprehend the escaping murders. His residence was attacked by a furious mob. In Varanasi there were riots.

Crowds, angry at Phoolan's assassination, which many blamed on the BJP, had to be dispersed by police. The rioters used stones, guns and crude bombs. Buses were torched and one man was killed. In Lucknow, police booths were set on fire and roads blocked. In Mirzapur, there were attacks on vehicles and houses. A heavy police presence, augmented by the deployment of nine companies of the Provincial Armed Constabulary, prevented more serious violence.

There had been an unseemly wrangle over the funeral arrangements. Phoolan's mother and many of the family were in Delhi, so they wished to hold the funeral there. The Samajwadi Party, however, was determined to obtain the maximum political advantage from the murder, and wanted the funeral to be held in her constituency of Mirzapur. The only way for the family to reach Mirzapur in time for the ceremony was to travel by chartered plane. The party chiefs had hired a small plane for themselves and Umed, but there was no room for the rest of the family. At one stage, Phoolan's mother threatened to set fire to herself. Eventually another plane was hired by the Samajwadi Party to transport the family.

The funeral was held at Mirzapur on the banks of that holy river of the Hindus, the Ganges. A large crowd started to assemble at the funeral ghat from dawn. Phoolan's mother, Moola, was at the ceremony that afternoon, as were Phoolan's three sisters, Rukhmani, Ramkali and Munni, and her brother, Shiv Narayan. Santosh and Mathura Prasad had come too. The Samajwadi Party was represented by its general secretary and its president, Mulayam Singh. Phoolan's body, garlanded with flowers and wrapped in the Samajwadi flag, was placed on top of the funeral pyre. Umed Singh applied the torch.

During that funeral day, Phoolan was constantly in my thoughts. I was at the library but hardly in the mood to concentrate on my work. My colleagues were most solicitous and there was a flood of emails from friends and acquaintances offering sympathy. I myself felt curiously detached. It seemed so unreal.

*

Newspapers around the world carried long obituaries. Most gave her age as thirty-seven. They focused on Phoolan's extraordinary transformation from bandit to law-maker. In Britain, *The Times* ran an editorial comparing her to Boadicea and Joan of Arc. The *Guardian* referred to her fighting valiantly 'for the poor and the downtrodden, the class into which she was born. She was even more ferocious in seeking gender equality and justice in a male-dominated society in which oppression and exploitation of women is egregious.' In India, the *Hindu*'s obituary noted that 'She had one regret – she felt that she still had a long way to go to ensure a life of dignity for the backward classes and a fair deal for the downtrodden.'

The President of India referred to Phoolan as 'the symbol of the struggle of the poorest of the poor and of the feminist crusade at its finest'.

*

The day after the funeral the police arrested their principal suspect, Sher Singh Rana. He was detained a hundred and forty miles north of Delhi in the Press Club at Dehradun. It was reported that he had been about to address a press conference but had been arrested before he could deliver his speech. The Indian press seemed to be unrestrained by the normal convention of writing anything that might prejudice a future trial. (Perhaps this was permitted because there were no juries in India. The judiciary had a touching faith in their own incorruptibility and impartiality, not always borne out by events.) Some reports, for example, said that Rana had told some of the journalists present that he had killed Phoolan to avenge the massacre at Behmai.

He was quoted by the Press Trust of India as saying, 'I am proud of what I have done. It was in my mind for quite some time.'

Sher Singh Rana was a somewhat bizarre character. It seemed that he was a law student in his early twenties. He was also joint proprietor of a liquor store in Haridwar. Three years before his arrest he had stood as a candidate in a Dehradun college student-union election. It was said that to increase his chance of winning he had faked his own kidnapping to get a sympathy vote. Rana was a Rajput, of the same Kshatriya caste division as those who were killed at Behmai. The *New York Times* reported on 28 July 2001 how, before surrendering at the Dehradun Press Club, he said that he had two ambitions in life. One was to kill Phoolan. The other was to go to Afghanistan to retrieve the remains of the twelfth-century Rajput ruler Prithviraj Chauhan. He was quoted as saying, 'If I am implicated, it is all right. I feel that with this act, the stigma of the Rajputs has been cleared.'

After his arrest, Sher Singh Rana was transferred to Delhi for interrogation. It seemed that he had abandoned his getaway car and then taken an auto-rickshaw to a bus station. From there, he had travelled to Haridwar and then proceeded to Dehradun. Guns had been found in the vehicles as well as in the garden of 44 Ashok Road. It was reported that under intensive questioning Rana had named three accomplices. These were then arrested at Saharanpur, between Delhi and Dehradun, and brought to Delhi for questioning. Umed Singh was also interrogated.

The police were reported to have established that on the morning of the assassination, Phoolan had been driven to parliament by Rana. She knew him as a friend of Uma Kashyap, who had arrived in Delhi with him the previous evening. Uma Kashyap was a long-established associate of Phoolan. She had been very active in Phoolan's non-political organisation, the Eklavya Sena. Like Phoolan, she came from the Mallah fishing caste. Phoolan had appointed her head of the Eklavya Sena in Roorkee, near Haridwar. After the assassination, interrogation of Uma Kashyap and her husband had revealed the role of Sher Singh Rana in Phoolan's murder.

As a result of all these interrogations, the police eventually charged Sher Singh Rana and ten associates with murder, conspiracy to murder or the destruction of evidence. Although the media seemed to think that the police had been successful in arresting the actual assassins, there was much speculation as to whether the murder had been instigated by more powerful figures. In particular, there was speculation that politicians were involved. There were rumours that Phoolan might have been planning to leave the Samajwadis for another party and that this might have alarmed the Samajwadi leadership.

A week after the assassination, there were sensational reports of clashes between Phoolan's blood family and her husband, Umed Singh. He had called a press conference at 44 Ashok Road. It was to announce the formation of a trust to administer Phoolan's assets 'for the upliftment of the downtrodden'. He claimed that Phoolan's family had backed this venture. However, those relatives present immediately attacked the plan. They alleged that Umed had married Phoolan to get hold of her property. Phoolan's younger sister, Munni, accused Umed of swindling Phoolan out of the money that she had received for *Bandit Queen*. 'How can he announce the creation of a trust?' she was reported to have said. 'He is the one who devoured Phoolan's earnings. How can he claim to be custodian of her family? We are her immediate family members and we know what Phoolan wanted.'

The crowded press conference then became even more heated. Phoolan's mother, Moola, said that ten days before the assassination Phoolan had told her that she was afraid that Umed Singh might have her killed in order to seize her property. 'She told me that Umed could kill her,' Moola was quoted as saying. 'She was so afraid that she avoided contact with him. She had even stopped sleeping with him because she thought he might wring her neck.'

Munni was equally direct. 'Umed is involved in the murder,' she was quoted as saying. She claimed that the day before the assassination Phoolan was planning to make a will that would exclude Umed. 'It seems that he came to know all about it.'

Umed Singh vigorously denied involvement in the murder. He said that the police had exonerated him from being in any way connected with the assassination. He would, he said, be entering politics to 'realise the dreams of Phoolan Devi'. He also mounted a strong personal attack on Munni, alleging that she was accusing him 'as her desire to get a share in the property was not fulfilled'.

Whatever the truth was about these claims and counter-claims, it seemed that all had not been well in the recent relationship between Phoolan and Umed. Kamini Jaiswal, Phoolan's lawyer, confirmed that Phoolan had been considering changing her will. She also said that Phoolan had filed a divorce petition that May. 'Phoolan was most disturbed with her husband.' This, of course, was very far from associating Umed with a conspiracy to murder. I was left shocked and disillusioned by the whole public circus. It robbed Phoolan of some of the dignity that she deserved in death.

A month after Phoolan's assassination another unsavoury claim was made on Phoolan's supposed wealth. Putti Lal, Phoolan's first husband, the man she had accused of opening her up with a knife to rape her when she was eleven, claimed that he was her sole heir. In a petition to a Kanpur court, he claimed to have been lawfully married to Phoolan under Hindu law and never to have been divorced.

*

I went to India six months after Phoolan's assassination. It was strange and sad for me, knowing that this time I would not be staying with her. I deliberately kept away from the places in the north that I associated with her. I spent most of my time in the south, where I visited tea estates to obtain material for my forthcoming book on the history of tea. I did, however, make a brief visit to Delhi.

I went to 44 Ashok Road. The house was almost bare. Phoolan's belongings were being moved out so as to vacate the official house for another occupant. There was, however, a little shrine to Phoolan with flowers around it and a lamp burning in front of her photograph. The sole residents were Munni, Hargobind and their two children. Fortunately for me, we managed to locate Sarfraaz to come and interpret. I was glad to learn that Putti Lal's claim on Phoolan's estate had collapsed. However, the family was still at war over her assets. Munni and Moola were still battling against Umed. He was being supported by various other family members. Relatives were constantly switching alliances. It sounded terrible and I resolved to stay clear of the family for the foreseeable future. I had happy memories of the past and did not want them to be destroyed by this feud.

When I asked when those accused of Phoolan's murder would be brought to trial, Munni told me that very little was happening. The prosecution seemed to have stalled. Moreover, she told me, she had heard that Sher Singh Rana was boasting that he would soon be released on bail. When I expressed incredulity at this, she said it all went to confirm that he had powerful backers.

While in Delhi, I engaged a lawyer to try and recover the two lakhs that I had sent to Phoolan for the purchase of the house in Chitrakut. This case dragged on for several years, cost me a considerable amount in fees and I never recovered the money.

*

A year after the murder, there was little sign of progress in bringing the accused to trial. The first judge to hear argument on the framing of charges was transferred. A new judge began the hearing all over again. As one of the defence advocates observed, 'At this pace, it will take a long time before the charges are actually framed.'

A year later, Sher Singh Rana and his fellow accused were still confined in Tihar, Delhi's high-security jail. The trial had still not commenced. This delay, I knew, was not unusual in India. As I had seen happen to Phoolan, a murder case could languish for many years.

On 17 February 2004, Sher Singh Rana escaped from Tihar Jail. At 7 a.m. a man in police uniform had come to the jail and identified himself as Arvind Kumar of the Delhi Armed Police. He produced a warrant authorising the production of Rana before a court in Haridwar in a case under the Gangsters Act. As a policeman was expected, the formalities were soon completed. Kumar asked for and received the forty rupees 'ration money', which was allowed for Rana's food. He then handcuffed Rana and took him away. At 7.45 a.m. the real policeman arrived to collect Rana. A reward of 50,000 rupees was offered for his recapture.

There were reports that soon after his escape Sher Singh Rana had telephoned his brother, and after telling him he was unhappy at the help he had received from him so far, told him to arrange delivery of two lakhs of rupees or face the consequences. The police were watching all Rana's known haunts. Ten days after the escape the police arrested the man they alleged had posed as the bogus policeman. Another associate was arrested, as was the real Arvind Kumar who, it seemed, was a genuine former constable in the Delhi Armed Police. Rana himself seemed to have vanished.

In April, Sher Singh Rana's father died. Rana telephoned his family when he heard the news, and the police traced the call back to a town in Bihar. Afterwards it was suggested that he was living in remote parts of Uttar Pradesh and Bihar, but taking care to keep moving so as to avoid recapture. He was believed to be receiving help from fellow members of his upper caste. In June, the trial of those accused together with Sher Singh Rana resumed without him.

Nothing more was heard of Rana for two years. On 24 April 2006, after a tip-off, the Delhi Police rearrested him in Kolkata. He was flown to Delhi for interrogation. The following day the police commissioner called a press conference. It seemed that after his escape Rana had checked into a hotel in a town in Uttar Pradesh. Relatives had sent him money. He had then used the services of a dubious passport agent in Ranchi to apply for a passport under the alias Sanjay Kumar Gupta. While waiting two months for this passport, Rana had visited Varanasi, where he obtained further funds from a backer who was confined there in the jail. When his passport arrived, Rana went to Kolkata to apply for a Bangladesh visa.

In Bangladesh, the commissioner said, Rana had rented a house. From time to time he had returned to Kolkata to renew his Bangladesh visa. From Bangladesh he had then flown to Dubai, and from there on to Afghanistan. In Afghanistan he travelled from Kabul to Ghazni to search for the grave of the Rajput king Prithviraj Chauhan. Rana had claimed to have found the grave, dug it up one night and exhumed some of his medieval hero's remains. These he had bagged up and couriered to a friend in India. He had then returned, via Dubai, to Bangladesh. He had been arrested in Kolkata while on a visit to renew his Bangladesh visa. A man of many aliases, he had checked into a hotel under the name of the assistant commissioner of the Delhi Police who had led his interrogation.

The media also reported that Rana had been desperate to stop Uma Kashyap, who was reported to have introduced him to Phoolan, from giving crucial evidence. She was scheduled to depose before the court in Delhi the following month. Police sources were quoted as saying that Rana had contacted a relative in Roorkee, Uma Kashyap's hometown, to ask him to find contract killers. Two known criminals had agreed to eliminate her for a fee of 150,000 rupees. One-third of this had been paid into the bank account of one of the potential assassins on the very day that Rana had been arrested in Kolkata. The pair were arrested on 2 May and taken to Delhi for interrogation.

Meanwhile, the Kshatriya Samaj, an organisation from Rana's caste, announced that it would be honouring him 'for upholding the dignity of the community as he has avenged the killing of twenty Kshatriyas in the Behmai massacre'. A spokesman said that Rana had displayed 'exemplary courage' by escaping from Tihar Jail and evading the police for two years. 'Such a person can be a role model for the young generation.'

Once safely back in Delhi, the trial of Rana and his associates got under way again. Progress, however, was painfully slow. The prosecution was calling a huge number of witnesses and many of these were being cross-examined. Phoolan's sister Munni, for example, was only called to give evidence over a year later, in September 2007. She was the prosecution's hundred and fourth witness and there were over a hundred more yet to testify.

In court Munni continued to claim that Umed Singh was behind the murder, although, of course, it was not him on trial. She also accused Uma Kashyap and her own nephew, Santosh, of being involved. I was terribly shocked that Santosh, who Phoolan had chosen to help me in my quest to find the Great Hedge of India, and who had been so helpful to me, was being dragged into the mire. And this was being done by Munni, one of my favourites in the family, the woman who had taken so much trouble to cook for me the foods that I liked.

More importantly, perhaps, Munni now insisted that she had not identified Sher Singh Rana as one of the assassins. In a statement to the police immediately after the murder, she had been recorded as saying that the 'monkey cap' of an assailant had slipped and that she had recognised him as Rana. Now she retracted this, and claimed that the assailant's face had been covered. The judge declared her a hostile witness. In the December, another key prosecution witness turned hostile. A personal assistant of Phoolan's withdrew his previous deposition that he had recognised Rana at the shooting and claimed that the assailants were, in fact, 'muffled up'. A year later, yet another key prosecution witness turned hostile. He had originally told the police that while offering prayers at a nearby shrine he had seen Rana and others fire at Phoolan. In court, however, he now denied that he had seen Rana.

*

In January 2009, perhaps as a result of the prosecution setbacks as its key witnesses changed their evidence, Sher Singh Rana's lawyers made an application to the High Court to have the case transferred to a 'fast-track court'. These courts were intended to take forward cases that had dragged on for over seven years. (That February, the Chief Justice of the Delhi High Court reported that given current resources, his court's backlog of 74,599 cases would take four hundred and sixty-six years to clear.) In a fast-track court, unlike in other courts, the judge had time available to expedite a particular case. On 21 January the Phoolan Devi murder case was moved to a fast-track court before a fresh judge, B. K. Garg. He announced that the trial would restart with regular hearing from 5 February. It looked as though the case, which had been in court since 2001, would now proceed relatively quickly.

It so happened that entirely by coincidence I flew into Delhi, a city I had rarely visited over recent years, two days after the fast-track court began sitting. I decided to go and see if I could observe proceedings. The court sat at Patiala House, an old palace of the maharajas of Patiala replete with decorated domes. I arrived there on the morning of 10 February. Given the importance of the case, I was expecting some grand courtroom. I was directed to 'No. 1 Evening Court', which was deserted. It was a tiny room, no more than twenty-five feet square with a ten-foot-high ceiling of polystyrene. About half the room was taken up by the crudely painted and massive judge's bench, with its two 'wings' for the dock and the witness box. A small space in front of the bench left just enough room for two rows of six chairs each. A clerk arrived and told me that proceeding would commence at ten thirty. I gathered that I was free to attend.

In the courtyard in front of the building there were stalls dispensing tea and snacks. The vendors were doing brisk business with a multitude of lawyers. Mostly men, they were easily recognisable as advocates by their black jackets, black or white trousers and white legal collars. These clothes were generally ill fitting and badly cut, giving their occupants an air of seediness. The advocates were, however, very affable. Soon they were asking me why I was there. Was I with the press? I told them I was an old friend of Phoolan's and they were surprisingly sympathetic. They assured me that the case would now move quickly to its conclusion. The judge in charge was famous for the speed with which he moved bogged-down cases forward. Also he was totally incorruptible. This combination of efficiency and honesty, they told me forcefully, was by no means common in India.

When I returned to the courtroom, it was filling up. Police brought in the defendants. Exactly how many of them were there I never worked out since, in addition to the four principal accused, there were various others who had been charged with providing false alibis and other assistance. It was difficult to sort out the defendants from the other attendees. The four main accused, however, were each accompanied by a policeman. As was normal in India, except when considered likely to escape, they were not handcuffed but were holding hands with their police escorts. This seemed rather surprising to me since Rana had previously escaped from custody and there was only a single man with a rifle guarding the outer door. I myself was neither searched nor asked to explain my presence until the end of the session. There seemed to be no press. Neither was there anyone from Phoolan's family.

The court rose for Judge Brijesh Garg. He was perhaps in his forties, with his smooth oiled black hair showing occasional flecks of grey. He had a neat moustache, wore gold-rimmed spectacles and had a pleasant manner. His voice was soft but authoritative.

Sher Singh Rana went into the dock. Now about thirty years old, he was short and slightly built. He had a moustache and a closely cropped beard. His short hair lengthened over his forehead into a fringe. He wore a bright orange zipped jumper over a bright green shirt. As various witnesses gave evidence, he would often give a dazzling smile and looked full of confidence. Then suddenly this would evaporate, to be replaced by a frown and a nervous unhappy look. At those moments, he would slowly pass his tongue over his lips.

The session was taken up with the formal identification of various sealed packets containing videotapes, DVDs and suchlike. 'Pointing out memos' from police witnesses were submitted by a woman lawyer for the prosecution and then labelled 'Exhibit W112/A' or something similar. It was not surprising that the press had failed to attend. Judge Garg directed matter with speed and efficiency. He spoke first in Hindi for the benefit of the defendant, and then in English for the court stenographer.

Before I left, a lawyer sitting next to me took it into his head to introduce me to the man on his other side. I found myself shaking hands with this man as the lawyer introduced him proudly as 'Sher Rana's brother'. Realising that he was one of those on trial, I hurriedly extricated my hand. Then, looking up, I saw Sher Singh Rana give me his dazzling smile.

Afterword

Brijesh Garg, the judge in the trial of Sher Singh Rana and his co-accused for the murder of Phoolan Devi, was replaced later in 2009 by yet another judge. Thereafter the trial lost momentum once again. At the beginning of 2010, the trial that had started in 2001 was still in progress. The defence lawyers had yet to produce their witnesses and it was still unclear what line their arguments for the defence would take.

Author's Note

During the time that I knew Phoolan Devi, I had no intention of writing about her. When we first made contact, I had no plans to become a writer. Although Phoolan met many other foreigners, they were nearly all writers or journalists. She was always a bit wary of these. The whole basis of my relationship with her was that I was not probing for information to publish and that I could be relied upon for support and to give her disinterested advice. When I did start writing *The Great Hedge of India*, in which she had a role, I masked her identity.

I was always aware, however, that Phoolan would be a historical figure. In order to preserve an account of her life that future historians might use to balance information from other sources, I kept copious records of events. I was already composing a daily diary (I have a pile of A4 pads going back over thirty years and several feet high) and made sure that my dealings with Phoolan were fully recorded. In addition, I kept special notebooks on all my visits to India. I kept copies of all correspondence. (The letters in Hindi have recently been translated by a professional translator, whose version I have used to produce an accurate text.) I also collected hundreds of relevant newspaper cuttings and took many photographs.

This book is compiled from these sources, augmented by what I can remember. I am well aware that my memory, like that of most of us, is liable to play tricks. In addition, my lack of knowledge of Indian customs and language may well have led to my misunderstanding some incidents. I have done my best to recreate events and dialogue as I recorded or remember them and hope that any errors will be forgiven as having been made in good faith.

Acknowledgements

As will be clear from reading the book, I am indebted to many people in both Britain and India for their help and hospitality. I am most grateful to them.

Three books about Phoolan Devi have been particularly useful:

Devi – The Bandit Queen by Richard Shears and Isobelle Gidley (London: George Allen & Unwin, 1984).

India's Bandit Queen – The True Story of Phoolan Devi by Mala Sen (London: Harvill, 1991).

I, Phoolan Devi – The Autobiography of India's Bandit Queen, with Marie-Thérèse Cuny and Paul Rambali (London: Little, Brown, 1996), originally published as *Moi, Phoolan Devi, Reine des Bandits* (Paris: Fixot, 1996).

I am also grateful to the various media organisations that I have cited. An authoritative translation of the Hindi letters made by Archana Verma, teacher of Hindi in the University of Delhi, was most helpful.

I should like to thank Nick Barnard, Jessica Moxham Lynch and Helen Armitage for reading through the original manuscript of this book and for their comments. I am also grateful to Judith Kendra, Sue Lascelles and Mel Yarker at Rider for their many useful suggestions.

Index